CONCEPTS AND TECHNIQUES IN MODERN GE

THE U.K. CENSUS OF POPULATION

by

J.C. Dewdney
(University of Durham)

CONTENTS

		page
I	INTRODUCTION	3
II	PREPARATIONS FOR THE 1981 CENSUS	3
III	THE CENSUS SCHEDULE	5
IV	PROCESSING THE DATA	7
V	THE POPULATION BASE	8
VI	CENSUS AREAS	9
VII	THE PUBLISHED DATA	10
	(i) Small Area Statistics	11
	(ii) The published volumes	14
	(iii) Supplementary documents	23
VIII	COMPARABILITY, 1971-1981	24
	(i) Changes in the population base	25
	(ii) Changes in the areal base	25
	(iii) Changes in the classifications used	28
	(iv) Changes in the variables used and their arrangement in tables	29
	(v) OPCS User Guide 84	29
IX	POST-CENSUS CHECKS	30
NOTES		31
REFERENCES		36
APPENDICES		38

APPENDICES

1. The census schedule, 1981: England — 38

2. Census schedules 1981 for Scotland, Wales and
   Northern Ireland — 45

3. Types and numbers of areas for which 1981 census
   data have been produced — 48

4. Standard format of the 1981 Small Area Statistics — 50

5. Published volumes of the 1981 census, Great Britain — 60

6. Census 1981, England and Wales: Standard tables of
   the County Reports — 62

7. Census 1981: OPCS County, Parliamentary Constituency,
   Ward and Civil Parish Monitors — 66

8. The OPCS Census Monitor series — 69

9. OPCS Monitor series — 70

10. The OPCS Census Topics series — 70

11. SAS 1971-81 Change File tables — 71

ACKNOWLEDGEMENTS

The preparation of this CATMOG would not have been possible without the
whole-hearted cooperation of the Office of Population Censuses and Surveys
and their colleagues in Scotland and Northern Ireland. In addition to
providing the copyright material in Appendices 4 & 11, the census offices
commented in detail on the draft text, supplied the answers to numerous
queries and provided me with a wide range of documents and other material.
Special thanks are due to Mr. C. Denham, Census Division, OPCS, for his
assistance at all stages. I must, of course, make it clear that any
remaining errors and omissions are entirely my own responsibility.

J.C.D.

I INTRODUCTION

An earlier booklet in this series (Dewdney, 1981), while primarily concerned with the scope and content of the 1971 census of the United Kingdom, also presented background information on such matters as the history of the census, the legal provisions under which it operates and the way in which it is organised. Except in instances where the situation in 1981 was significantly different from that in earlier censuses, or where it is felt that additional information might be of value to census users, this background material is not repeated here and the reader requiring more detail is referred to the earlier CATMOG and to more recent publications describing the census (e.g. Rhind, 1983).

The main intention of the present CATMOG is to provide a concise guide to the 1981 census. With this end in view, the main body of the text has purposely been kept fairly general and the more detailed information is relegated to a set of <u>Notes</u> (pp.31 - 36) and some extensive <u>Appendices</u> (pp.38 - 75). The latter, it is hoped, will be of assistance to the census user in his search for the data appropriate to his needs. In addition to describing the census held on 5/6 April, 1981, this CATMOG shows how the 1981 census differs from its predecessors, and particularly from the 1971 version, and discusses some of the problems which arise from these differences (see especially Section VIII).

The fact that the U.K. census continues to be carried out separately by, though with a good deal of collaboration between, the three Census Offices[1] responsible for England and Wales, Scotland and Northern Ireland respectively presents problems both to the census user with interests which cover the U.K. as a whole and to the writer of this CATMOG. The space available does not allow a definitive treatment of all three sections of the United Kingdom, and attention is inevitably centred on the most populous - England and Wales - which contains 87.7 per cent of the 'British' population.[2] Nevertheless, some attempt is made to indicate where practices in Scotland and/or Northern Ireland diverge from those in England and Wales and to explain at least the major differences between the three countries.

II PREPARATIONS FOR THE 1981 CENSUS

Planning for the 1981 census began almost five years before census day, and involved both a greater measure of consultation with potential users and the publication of a larger volume of explanatory and publicity material than on previous occasions. Potential census users were consulted through three advisory committees - one each for government departments, for local authorities and for research councils and learned societies (OPCS, 1977) and contact was made with a variety of other organisations. Several provisional decisions were made at a very early stage, notably the use of the same questionnaire for all private households,[3] the use wherever possible of multiple-choice questions to be answered by the tick-box method and the omission of any questions directly related to fertility.[4] It was also proposed to replace the 1971 question on parents' birthplace by "a direct question on each person's ethnic group", a suggestion which aroused

3

considerable opposition and controversy. A steady stream of detailed information on proposals for the census was provided by a series of OPCS Monitors,[5] the first of which was published early in 1978, and January 1981 saw the appearance of the first of a series of Census Topics,[6] information sheets "aimed at the enquiring layman". The Monitor series continued after the census had taken place and reports the publication of results and other post-census activities. Similar documents were produced by the census authorities in Scotland and Northern Ireland.

The Parliamentary process without which no British census can take place was initiated by the July 1978 'White Paper' 1981 Census of Population (Cmnd 7146). The appearance of this document nearly three years before census date took place "because the Government believe that there should be time for public discussion and because it is important that firm instructions should be given early to the census planners" if delays such as those experienced in the publication of the 1971 results were to be avoided.[7]

The White Paper reiterated "certain broad principles" on which the proposals for the census were based, namely that it "should be confined to obtaining information for which there is a real need and which will be put to good use", that it "should be acceptable to the public by respecting their privacy and limiting its demands" and that it "should meet the essential needs of census-users as rapidly and flexibly as cost will allow". (The cost of the 1981 operation was estimated at £45 million - November 1976 prices - equivalent to about 90 pence per head of the total population). The White Paper also discussed the matters of confidentiality, consultation with potential users, the topics to be covered, the sample surveys to be carried out before and after the census proper and the ways in which the census was to be conducted and its results published.

Following extensive consultation with prospective users, the draft Census Order 1980 (S.I. 1980/702) related to the taking of the census in Great Britain was laid before both Houses of Parliament by the Secretary of State for Social Services on 20 March 1980, as stipulated by the Census Act, 1920, under which all censuses since that date have been held. The Order was debated in the House of Lords on 22 April 1980, and again on 6 May 1980 (Hansard, vol. 408, 116, 123) following a debate in the Commons on 29 April 1980 (Hansard, vol. 983, 165). These debates resulted in several amendments to the draft Order, notably the reinstatement of a question on vehicle ownership, which had been omitted from the original proposals, and the final removal of the proposed 'ethnic' question. The last matter had already provoked vigorous debate, both in Parliament and elsewhere, and a government decision to drop the idea was announced in advance of the debates on the draft Order.

As already indicated, the census authorities, in England and Wales at least, had favoured an ethnic question on the grounds that it would "yield a better measure of ethnicity than, as in 1971, reliance on information on country of birth and parents' country of birth, because by 1981 there (would) be many more members of ethnic minorities themselves born in Britain and having parents, too, born in Britain". The aim of the question would be "to provide an objective measure of the numbers and conditions - housing, employment and so on - of the main ethnic groups" (OPCS, 1977, 8). Considerable effort was expended by OPCS in devising a suitable ethnic question for inclusion in the 1981 census and OPCS carried out sample surveys, using a

4

variety of such questions in a variety of areas between 1975 and 1978
(Sillitoe, 1978a, b, c). Following representations from a various bodies,
it was eventually decided to exclude not only the proposed ethnic question
but also those asked in 1971 on parents' birthplaces and on year of entry
into the U.K. and to exclude any question on nationality.

On this contentious issue it is intriguing to note that OPCS considered
it necessary to produce some of their publicity material in Bengali,
Cantonese, Greek, Gujerati, Hindi, Italian, Punjabi and Turkish and to provide translations of the census questions into those languages for use in
certain areas. Following the completion of the 1981 census, the Sub-
Committee (of the House of Commons Home Affairs Committee) on Race Relations
and Immigration carried out an enquiry into whether or not there should be
an ethnic question in the next census. The sub-committee recommended that
such a question should be asked and that in addition, questions on language
spoken and ability to speak English should also be included.

Following these amendments, the final version of the Order in Council
was signed by H.M. the Queen on 21 May 1980 and the Census Regulations 1980
(S.I. 1980/897) were made by the Secretary of State on 30 June 1980. Similar
regulations were produced for Scotland and Northern Ireland.

Meanwhile, recruitment of staff to carry out the census operations had
proceeded along the usual lines (Dewdney, 1981, 7) involving, for England and
Wales, a labour force of about 120 000 - 110 Census Supervisors, 2100 Census
Officers, 6400 Assistant Census Officers and about 112 000 Enumerators,
together with a large temporary clerical staff at OPCS to assist in processing the data. Although the details of organization were somewhat different in England and Wales, Scotland and Northern Ireland respectively, the
post and duties of the Enumerator were common to all three countries and it
was the Enumerator who was responsible for the great bulk of the census
field operation over a period of four to five weeks. The Enumerator's duties
involved the identification and listing of all households[8] within his
Enumeration District (ED), the delivery to each household of an advance
publicity leaflet, followed by the census questionnaire or 'schedule', the
collection and checking of the schedules (with return visits to errant households where necessary) and the provision of a preliminary count of the
population of the ED for use in the preparation of the census Preliminary
Reports.

III THE CENSUS SCHEDULE

A full list of the questions asked in 1981 of all private households in
England[9] is given in Appendix 1, pages 38 - 44 which also indicates where
these differed significantly from the questions asked in 1971.[10] Appendix
2, pages 45-47, shows the main differences between the questions asked in
England and those used in other parts of the United Kingdom.

While the number of questions asked was reduced from 29 (five household
and 24 population questions) in 1971 to 21 (five household and 16 population
questions) in 1981, the reduction in the total amount of information
collected was less than these figures might suggest since, in the answers to
several questions, more detail was required than on previous occasions.

5

A number of questions asked in 1971 were absent from the 1981 schedule. As already indicated, the latter omits any questions on fertility (questions B23, B24 in 1971). In the case of household amenities, (qn. A5 in 1971, H3 in 1981), cooker, kitchen sink and hot water supply were no longer included, presumably on the grounds that there is no longer a significant number of households lacking such basic amenities. In Northern Ireland, however (Appendix 2), a much wider range of information of this type was collected, including details of water supply, sewerage provision, the type of fuel used and the presence or absence of central heating and roof and/or wall insulation. In Scotland, additional details of the household's accommodation were required (see below).

More serious from the point of view of the census user - and particularly the population geographer - was the reduction in the amount of data collected concerning migration movements. Whereas the 1971 schedule asked for 'usual address' both one year and five years prior to the census (1971 qns. B11, B12), the 1981 schedule asks only for "usual address one year ago". This change was largely the result of economic considerations - it halved the very large volume of work involved in the cross-tabulation of addresses to produce the migration tables - though part of this saving was lost by the decision to code migration on a 100% basis instead of from only 10% of the schedules as in previous censuses.[11] Thus the 1981 migration data are more accurate than on previous occasions, but relate only to moves during a single twelve-month period.

Other significant omissions were the absence of a question on the number of hours worked per week (qn. B19 in 1971)[12], and on change of occupation in the year previous to the census (qn. B22 in 1971).

Attention has already been drawn to the contentious matter of the ethnic origins of the British population and to the arguments which led to the abandonment not only of the proposed "direct question about ethnicity" but also of the questions asked in 1971 on parents' birthplaces (qn. B10) and date of entry into the U.K. (qn. B9b). As a result of these decisions, the 1981 census provides even less information than its predecessors on ethnicity, language, religion or other 'cultural' characteristics of the population.[13] There is no information on ethnic origin or affiliation save that provided indirectly and incompletely by the question on 'country of birth' (1981 qn. 9), which is even less satisfactory than in the past, now that many members of ethnic minorities have been born in the U.K.[14] Questions on language are confined to the special cases of Welsh and Scottish Gaelic in Wales and Scotland respectively (Appendix 2, pages 45-47) and religious affiliation is recorded only in Northern Ireland, and then only partially since this is a voluntary question (the only such question in the British census).[15]

Elsewhere, however, the amount of information recorded has considerably increased, mainly as a result of the addition of new categories to classifications used on previous occasions. This applies particularly in the cases of the questions on tenure (1981 qn. H2), marital status (qn. 4), employment status (qns. 10, 13) and mode of travel to work (qn. 15).

The data collected concerning the physical nature of the household's accommodation has also been expanded by a revision of the details to be filled in on each schedule by the Enumerator. This is particularly true of

6

Scotland where, *inter alia*, detached, semi-detached and terraced dwellings and blocks of flats with 2, 3 or 4 and 5 or more storeys - with or without lifts - are distinguished, along with the 'actual floor of entry' to households accommodated on the first or higher floors. The wide range of information on amenities collected in Northern Ireland has already been mentioned.

These features, together with certain differences in question wording and in the general format of the household schedules as between England and Wales, Scotland and Northern Ireland, reflect the continuing compartmentalisation of the U.K. census. Differences occur not only in the details of the data collected, but also in the way in which they are published (see below, Section VII).

Other, less important changes may also be noted. The increased use of tick-boxes and a consequent reduction in the amount of information to be written in by the respondent reduces the possibilities for erroneous or ambiguous answers and speeds the processes of coding and manipulating the data (Dewdney, 1981, 12-14). Social pressures are reflected in the matter of the individual responsible for completing the household schedule. In 1971, the schedule was addressed to "the Head or Acting Head of the Household"; in 1981 this underwent a subtle change to "the Head or Joint Heads or Members of the Household" (in Scotland, however, "Head, Joint Heads or Acting Head" was used). In 1971, the first question (B1) asking for the name of each individual was to be answered first by "the head of household (if present)", who thus became the 'first person' on the schedule for whom the data were to be provided. Question B5 required the description "Head" for the first person on the schedule and other members of the household were required to state their 'relationship to the head of household'. In 1981, the equivalent question (5) asked for 'relationship in household' and each person was required to state his or her "relationship to the person entered in the first column". Despite this attempt to get round the objections of respondents to whom the term "Head of Household" was obnoxious, the term appears frequently in the published results and has had to be carefully defined for this purpose by OPCS.[16]

IV PROCESSING THE DATA

Though the computer techniques used in 1981 were more sophisticated and more speedy, the general procedures involved in processing the data which were described in our previous publication (Dewdney, 1981, 12-14) also applied in 1981 and details of these procedures are not repeated here. Information on the production of data files, the way in which these files were used to create the published output and how this affected the order in which the published material appeared are to be found in OPCS (1978) and (Rhind 1983, 36-41). Such matters are of marginal interest to the census user now that the results have been published. We turn, therefore, to various aspects of the publication of the 1981 data.

7

V THE POPULATION BASE

One major change instituted in the 1981 census requires special mention since it presents considerable problems to census users wishing to make comparisons between the 1981 and earlier censuses (see Section VIII). For all British censuses up to and including 1971, individual records were aggregated to areal units on a *de facto* basis, that is each individual was allocated to the area in which he or she happened to be present on census night.[17] In 1981, although this long-established system was not wholly abandoned and simple tables of 'persons present' were produced for all areas, the bulk of the tables were produced on a modified[18] *de jure* system. An individual was recorded as 'present and usually resident' or 'absent and usually resident' (where someone else was present to fill in the schedule), or as a 'visitor' (giving usual address): this was the basis of allocation to two population bases for each area - the 'population present' (on census night) and the 'usually resident' population.

The great majority of published tabulations refer to the 'usually resident'. This change from a *de facto* to a *de jure* population base was undertaken primarily in response to the wishes of local government officials, who constitute the biggest single group of census users and who made the wholly valid point that they were concerned mainly with the population usually resident within their Local Authority Areas rather than with those who happened to be present there on the occasion of the census.

This matter of the population base is, however, more complex than the simple statement above would suggest and requires further explanation. As already indicated, there are two distinct but overlapping populations of a given area (A) - the population present in that area on census night, used for the majority of tabulations in censuses down to 1971, and the 'usually resident' population, used in 1981. Visitors to area A on census night whose usual residence is outside that area are included in the 'population present' but excluded from the 'usually resident' total. This presents no problems, but difficulties arise in the case of individuals usually resident in area A but absent from that area on census night. Such individuals should, in theory, all be included in the 'usually resident' population. They may be counted in two different ways:

(i) from the entries on census schedules filled in for households in area A giving details for all persons usually resident at that address; or, alternatively:

(ii) from the entries on census schedules filled in for households outside area A recording the presence of individuals whose usual address is in area A; the records for such individuals can, in theory, be transferred for inclusion in the totals for area A. (This is the 'transfer method'; see Definitions, OPCS 1981).

The effort involved in tracking down residents of Area A whose particulars appear on schedules filled in outside area A and adding them to the totals for area A (the transfer method (ii) above) would clearly be very great and no final figures for area A could be produced until the schedules for all other areas (i.e. for the entire U.K.) had been processed. Such a procedure would have resulted in unacceptable delays in the publication of the census results; consequently, the totals of 'usually resident' population

8

which appear in such publications as the County Monitors and County Reports (see Section VII) omit some of this 'transfer' category (i.e. those absent from households in which there was no one present to complete a schedule). Thus they represent, for each area, a count of persons recorded on census schedules from that area as usually living 'at this address', whether or not they were present on census night, excluding visitors whose usual address was in another area and including 'absent residents', providing that there was somebody present in the household to record their absence. It follows that, if an entire household were absent, all its members were omitted from the count.

It should be noted that the count of 'usually resident' population in census publications differs from that used by the Registrar-General in his Annual Estimates for Local Authority and other areas. These do include persons transferred from other areas by method (ii) above. In addition, the Registrar-General's estimates adopt a different convention from the census in the case of students, members of the armed forces and some other categories. A student's 'usual address', for example, is taken for the purposes of the Registrar-General's estimates as his term-time address, but for census purposes as his home address "because this is how most of the public respond best to the questionnaire" (Definitions, OPCS 1981, 5). It follows, regrettably, that the population counts in the two sources are not strictly comparable. More serious is the fact that the base population for 1981 census tabulations is not directly comparable with that used in the 1971 and earlier censuses (see Section VIII).

The various population bases for England and Wales in 1981 were as follows (to the nearest 10 000):

Population present, Preliminary Report figure	49.01 million
Population present, final figure	49.15 million
Usually resident population, transfer method	49.18 million
Usually resident population, present/absent method	48.52 million
Registrar-General's mid-year estimate	49.59 million

Apart from the mid-year estimate, which refers to a date some nine weeks after the census, these figures differ by barely 50 000, equivalent to 0.1 per cent of the population. Larger percentage differences occur for smaller areas and for particular categories of people.

VI CENSUS AREAS

As in 1971, 1981 census data were produced, either in the published volumes or as Small Area Statistics (see Section VII) for a wide variety of areal units, which included not only Enumeration Districts (EDs) and the various levels of the administrative hierarchy, but also units of other kinds such as Standard Regions, Parliamentary Constituencies and Regional Health Authorities. A full list of these territorial units appears in Appendix 3, pages 48-49.

Once again, there are significant differences between the constituent countries of the U.K. Some of these are inevitable, resulting from their different administrative structures; others are the result of decisions made by the various census offices, notably those concerned with the matter of postcode areas.

9

Postcodes form a unique areal reference system which covers all mail-receiving addresses in the U.K. and postcode areas, at first sight, appear to present an ideal areal base for the aggregation of many types of statistics, including the census data. They do, however, present certain difficulties, notably that they cannot always be aggregated to areal units whose boundaries coincide with those of Local Authority Areas (LAAs). Despite such difficulties, the General Register Office (Scotland) decided to form Scottish EDs by grouping unit postcodes, and the latter are split only where this was necessary in order to make ED boundaries coincide with the boundaries of LAAs and other statutory areas. Furthermore, in the Scottish case postcodes had been added to the addresses on the 1971 schedules and it was possible to recreate certain 1971 data to the 1981 ED base, thus aiding comparisons between the two censuses. In England and Wales, the use of postcodes in census geography was tested, but was found to cost more than the conventional approach, and the additional resources necessary to match the Scottish postcoding exercise were not available; consequently EDs were constructed without reference to postcode areas. However, unit postcodes were inserted by the enumerator on all census schedules and were attached to the records in data files of place of residence, workplace and address one year ago.[19] These postcodes were used in the preparation of migration, workplace and journey to work tables.

In both countries, the Enumeration District, arrived at somewhat differently in each case, remains the smallest areal unit for which census data are made available (through SAS) to the census user, and aggregates of ED data form the basis for tabulations at LAA and other levels in the published volumes. Problems of comparability between the 1981 and earlier censuses are considerable as a result of intervening changes in the various areal bases, and this applies particularly at the level of EDs which have, in effect, been designed afresh for each successive census. A primary constraint on the design of EDs is the requirement that they should not transgress administrative boundaries (which themselves change between censuses) so that ED data can be aggregated to Wards and thence to other levels of the administrative hierarchy.[20] Equally important is the requirement that EDs should "represent a workload that can be performed by the Enumerator in the time available, given the circumstances of the area" (Denham, 1980). In the event, only about 46 per cent of the 1981 EDs in England and Wales were precisely the same as those used in 1971. Special methods have been devised by OPCS to overcome this difficulty (see Section VIII).

VII THE PUBLISHED DATA

As in 1971, there are two basic forms in which 1981 census data are made available to the census user. The simpler and more easily accessible comprises the published volumes (see below, Section VII(ii)) which give a wide range of information tabulated for Local Authority Areas and other types of 'official' territorial divisions. A much greater body of material is contained in the Small Area Statistics (SAS), first produced for the whole of Great Britain in 1971 and greatly expanded in 1981. These are available either direct from the census offices or through a number of intermediate agencies (see below). In addition, special tabulations to the customer's design may be obtained from the census offices provided that the latter have the resources to carry out the computation involved.

(i) <u>Small Area Statistics (SAS)</u>

SAS comprise a standard set of tables which can be made available on magnetic tape, on microfilm, on microfiche or on paper, for Enumeration Districts, Electoral Wards (England and Wales) or Postcode Sectors (Scotland), local government Districts and all higher levels of the administrative hierarchy. Payment to the census offices is involved, but there are several 'communities of users' among whom SAS may be freely circulated once an initial payment has been made. These include Local Authorities, Health Authorities and the Universities and Polytechnics. In the latter case, a full set of SAS has been purchased by the ESRC (Economic and Social Research Council, formerly SSRC), and the magnetic tape version is mounted at a number of regional University computer centres. In addition, several commercial agencies have been established which are licensed to hold SAS and retail them to business and other private users on payment of royalties to the census offices. Dissemination and use of the 1981 SAS is likely to be much wider than in 1971, particularly as the 1981 set provides very much more detail. The 1981 SAS are subject to the same confidentiality restraints and the 'adjustment' and 'suppression' procedures as applied in 1971 (Dewdney, 1981, 15-16). Suppression is likely to affect only a very small proportion of the Enumeration Districts.

Standard 1981 SAS tables are reproduced in Appendix 4, pages 50-59. Each table (usually a group of cross-tabulations) has a header indicating the category or categories of persons or households to which it applies and each cell has a unique number for reference purposes. Thus 'derived variables' can be obtained from the raw data (counts) in the SAS tables by specifying the manipulation of individual cells: the author of this CATMOG has produced a set of 360 such variables,[21] details of which may be obtained from him on request.

Comparison of Appendix 4 with the 1971 version (Dewdney, 1981, 34-36) will indicate the great expansion which has occurred both in the number of tables (28 in 1971, 53 in 1981) and, more significantly, in the number of cells (i.e. counts) provided (fewer than 1600 in 1971, more than 5000 in 1981). Such a comparison will also reveal major changes in the layout of these tables, an aspect which requires further explanation.

The 1971 SAS covered three pages, labelled 100% Population, 100% Household and 10% Sample and were standard for the whole of Great Britain. The 1981 version covers ten pages, arranged as follows:
> Pages 1-4, Tables 1-32, cells 1-2597: 100% items[22], standard for the
> whole of Great Britain
> Pages 5-6, Tables 44-53, cells 4223-5517: 10% items, standard for the
> whole of Great Britain
Thereafter there is a division between the two countries:
> Pages 7-8, Tables 33-38, cells 2598-3050: 100% England and Wales only
> Table 39, cells 3051-3098: 100% Wales only
> Pages 9-10, Tables 40-43, cells 3099-4222: 100% Scotland only
As a result of this arrangement, table numbers do not follow the same sequence as page numbers (all 100% tables are numbered before 10% tables). Cell numbers follow the sequence of table numbers. The total number of cells for each country (compared with 1571 in 1971) can be calculated as follows:

11

| | Common | | Specific | Total |
	100%	10%	100%	
England	2597	1295	453	4345
Wales	2597	1295	501*	4393
Scotland	2597	1295	1124	5016

* 453 common with England

For the 130 047 Enumeration Districts, this gives a potential data set of
well over 500 million items (five times as many as in 1971) though in practice, of course, many of these will be zeroes. The magnetic tapes carry all
4345, 4393 or 5016 items, according to country, but not every cell appears in
the printed version. It is possible to identify the missing items in the
printed tables from the arrangement of the cell numbers: in Table 2, for
example, cell 50 is "total persons", cell 52 is "single, widowed and divorced
males" and cell 53 is "married males". The 'missing' cell 51 clearly refers
to "total males" and can be obtained by summing cells 52 and 53. Cells where
no value is likely to occur - "married males aged 0-4" in Table 2, for
example - are marked XXX, but the equivalent cell number (60 in this case) is
not used.[23]

The contents of the various tables may be summarized as follows: Page 1
gives basic population statistics. Table 1 distinguishes residents - present
and absent - from visitors, and gives the two population bases: 'all present'
and 'all resident' in the area. Tables 2 and 4 divide the resident population by age, sex, marital status and country of birth. Table 5 covers the
economic position of all adults (i.e. those aged 16 and over), Table 7 the
economic status of adults in employment and Table 9 the age, sex, marital
status and employment status of all economically active residents. Table 8
shows the 'one year migrants' aged 1 year or over by age, sex and marital
status.[24] Tables 3 and 6, unlike the others on this page, use the 'all
present' population base, giving details of its division between private and
non-private households. It is clear from this description, that the totals
in the various tables (e.g. cells 50, 210, 380, 450 etc.) are different from
each other and care must be taken when constructing derived variables from
more than one table to make the appropriate choice.

Page 2 is concerned mainly with the characteristics of households[25],
such as tenure, amenities, size (both persons per household and rooms per
household) and density (persons per room). In most cases, the tables are
concerned with households with residents at the time of the census, but
Tables 11 and 16 deal with special cases such as holiday homes and households
with no usually resident persons. Table 17 compares household sizes derived
from the two population bases. Note that, in the majority of cases, data
are given not only on the number of households in a particular category but
also on the number of people usually resident in such households. Thus, for
example, cell 971 in Table 10 tells us how many owner-occupied households
have neither a bath nor an inside W.C. and cell 979 records the number of
people usually resident in households of that type.

The tables on page 3 mainly give information on the characteristics of
the residents of private households such as their age, sex, marital status

and economic position. At first sight, there might appear to be an overlap or repetition of information provided on page 1 - Table 21, for example, looks very much like Table 2 and Table 20 is similar to Table 5. The table headings, however, point the difference - Tables 2 and 5 refer to all residents, Tables 20 and 21 apply to residents in private households only. Once again, care must be taken to distinguish between the two.

Several tables (18, 19, 22, 24) on page 3 give details of household composition: cell 1549 in Table 18, for example, indicates the number of households composed of a married male, a married female and two or more children below the age of five. This is the nearest approach in the SAS to a statement of family structure, but we cannot assume that such a group represents a family in the biological sense: the married male and married female are not necessarily married to each other and the children are not necessarily the children of both or even one of the two adults.

Data on household composition continue on page 4, which gives details of households likely to be of particular concern to the social services such as lone-parent families (Table 17: note the careful use of inverted commas around the word 'parent' for reasons explained above) and households with or wholly composed of pensioners (Table 32). Table 30 appears somewhat esoteric in indicating the amenities enjoyed by migrant households.

The 10% sample tables on pages 5 and 6 cover items where coding and cross-tabulation at the 100% level would have placed an intolerable burden on the census offices. The main items in this category are industrial class, socio-economic group and travel to work. Care must be taken in using such 10% data for genuinely 'small' areas. At ED level in particular, "10 per cent SAS tables are subject to large errors[26] and will generally need to be aggregated to much higher area levels to ensure small variability in the cell values. The statistics are presented at ED level primarily to allow flexible aggregation" (Rhind, 1983, 80).

Pages 7 and 8 are specific to England and Wales (Table 39 on page 8 to Wales alone). Page 7 deals with household spaces, the nature of their accommodation and whether it is self-contained or part of a building shared with other households, and cross-tabulates these features with amenities. In Scotland, these tables are replaced by those on pages 9 and 10, where extremely detailed information on the households' accommodation is cross-tabulated with household composition. As an example of the level of detail in this section of the Scottish SAS, cell 3358 in Table 41 gives the number of female pensioners aged 75 or over living alone in fifth- or sixth-floor accommodation to which there is access by means of a lift.

Page 8 provides, for England and Wales, some further information on households. This includes a number of items not tabulated for Scotland, notably the distinction between freehold and leasehold owner-occupied accommodation (Table 38), which does not apply under Scottish law, and the identification of households with heads born in the U.K., in the Irish Republic, in the New Commonwealth and Pakistan, or elsewhere (Tables 36, 37).

Finally, Table 39 on page 8 and Table 40 on page 10 are derived from answers to the language questions in Wales and Scotland respectively. Both these tables refer to the resident population aged 3 years or over.

A variety of maps have been produced for use with the 1981 SAS and are available, either as paper sheets or on microfilm, from the census offices or from the ESRC Data Archive. There is a complete national coverage at 1:10 000 or 1:50 000 scale showing the boundaries of Local Authority Areas and Wards, and at 1:10 000 scale showing Wards and Enumeration Districts (one map for each local government District). In addition, ED and Ward maps at larger scales (1:2500 and 1:1250) are available for those - mainly urban - areas where their use was necessary in planning Enumeration Districts. Postcode boundary maps have been produced for Scotland. Details of these and of the many written guides to the SAS and other census statistics may be obtained from the census offices.[27]

Since the advent of the first nationwide SAS in 1966 and their expansion to the first national 100% SAS in 1971, considerable effort has been devoted to the preparation of statistical packages for use with these data. The most important is SASPAC, produced specifically for the 1981 SAS by the Universities of Durham and Edinburgh under contract to the Local Authorities Management Services and Computer Committee (LAMSAC). SASPAC runs on many different makers' computers, produces straightforward analyses of the data and prepares data for input to more complex statistical and mapping packages. The most widely used mapping package is GIMMS, produced by Gimms Ltd. of Edinburgh. These aspects are well covered in the Census User's Handbook (Rhind, 1983).

(ii) The Published Volumes

A full set of the published volumes from the 1981 census for the whole of the United Kingdom comprises over 200 separately bound items containing approximately 18 000 pages of tables and costing in the region of £1400.[28] However, the summary statistics in OPCS Monitors (q.v.) may be obtained without charge (or at a modest charge for larger orders - for example, £40 for selected data for 22 000 Wards and Civil Parishes) and the Key Statistics volumes (q.v.) giving data for every local authority and urban area are moderately priced. Comparison with the equivalent details for 1971 (Dewdney, 1981, 17-22, 37-42) suggests that, in terms of volumes and pages - though not, unfortunately in terms of price - the 1981 output is considerably smaller. However, this results mainly from a reduction in the number of areal units for which data are provided, following the local government reorganisation of 1974/5, an event which reduced the number of Local Authority Areas in Great Britain from 1857 in 1971 to 518 in 1981.[29] The amount of information provided for each area was in fact much greater in 1981 than in 1971.

A full listing of the published volumes from the 1981 census is available from the annual HMSO catalogue Government Publications for the years 1981-1984 inclusive. A summary of the volumes available and the distribution of the data among them is attempted in Appendix 5, pages 60-61. A variety of areal bases are used in the published tables and these are also indicated in Appendix 5. Before commenting on these aspects, a number of general points may be made:

(1) In the case of the 1981 census it was decided to reduce to a minimum the amount of 'preliminary' and provisional material, based either on initial counts by the enumerators or on a sample of the census schedules, published in advance of the main results. This permitted the census offices to

concentrate their efforts, from an early stage, on producing the definitive volumes and to complete the publication programme much more rapidly than on previous occasions. Provisional material was therefore confined to the Preliminary Reports.(30)

(2) For the U.K. as a whole, the great bulk of the 1981 material has been published at the level of Counties (Regions in Scotland) and Districts. The irritating practice of 'thresholding' LAAs - i.e. omitting certain data for urban divisions with populations below 50 000 and for all rural districts (Dewdney, 1981, 18, 37-39) was abandoned. Whereas in 1971 a very limited amount of material for Wards and Civil Parishes was included in the County Reports, in 1981 a rather wider range of information was provided at that level, but was published separately in a set of OPCS Ward and Civil Parish Monitors(31) (see below).

(3) An innovation in 1981 was the publication, in parallel with the main results, of pamphlet series which either give a selection of the material also available in the main volumes (OPCS County Monitors in England and Wales, Regional Bulletins in Scotland) or present data at areal levels not covered in the main reports (the Ward and Civil Parish Monitors already mentioned, Parliamentary Constituency Monitors for Great Britain). Details of these publications are given in Appendix 7 pages 66-68. In addition to their publication in pamphlet form, County Monitors and Regional Bulletins are also reprinted in the appropriate County and Regional reports; a second set of Parliamentary Constituency Monitors containing 1981 data re-aggregated to 1983 boundaries is also available both in pamphlet form and as a single, bound volume.

(4) A major factor in the arrangement of all this material has been the distinction between variables derived from the coding of all census schedules (the 100% variables) and those derived from a 10% sample. OPCS has listed the questions from which these two sets of variables are derived as follows:

100% questions: nature of accommodation and sharing; number of rooms; household tenure; household amenities; availability of cars and vans; age; sex; marital status; whereabouts on census night; usual address one year ago; country of birth; Welsh/Gaelic language; activity last week; employment status.

10% questions: relationship in household; occupation; industry; workplace; means of transport to work; higher qualifications.

The way in which this dichotomy affects the Small Area Statistics has already been discussed (p.11 above); it has also been a major factor in the allocation of the census variables to the appropriate published volumes.

(5) The great variety of areal units for which the census data are made available is indicated in Appendix 3. Small Area Statistics are available for all these units, but in the case of the published volumes the situation is more complex. Here, a variety of aggregation levels are used for the presentation of data; in many cases, two or more different levels are used within a single volume. The intricacies of this system preclude a definitive statement within the confines of this CATMOG; however, in Appendix 5, where the published volumes are listed, the main levels of aggregation used in each volume are indicated by an 'aggregation code'. The code number in each case

indicates the lowest level at which data are presented; tabulations usually also include data at higher levels, e.g. for countries where figures are given for counties, for counties where they are given for districts. Where more than one code number appears, this indicates that different levels are used in different sets of tables. The main aggregation levels are:

1. Country level only: Great Britain, England and Wales, England, Wales, Scotland
2. Standard Region-based: Standard Regions, Metropolitan Counties, Regional remainders, Central Clydeside conurbation, Remainder of Scotland
3. County level: Counties of England and Wales, local government Regions and Islands Areas of Scotland
4. LAA level: Districts (including London Boroughs)
5. Ward level: Wards and Civil Parishes (Communities in Wales)
6. Postcode Sectors: in Scotland only
7. Special areas as indicated by the volume title

(6) As in 1971, the 1981 census publications may be divided into three main categories: preliminary reports, county volumes and 'national volumes'. This categorisation is used in Appendix 5 and forms the basis of the discussion which follows.

(a) Preliminary Reports The three Preliminary Reports - one each for England and Wales, Scotland and Northern Ireland - give counts, made by the enumerators, of the population present on census night and compare these with their equivalents in earlier censuses. In England, Wales and Northern Ireland, the data are given at County and District levels; the Scottish volume also gives figures for postcode sectors and 'localities'.**(32)**

Comparisons of population counts with those from earlier censuses are carried further in the Historical Tables 1801-1981 published separately for England and Wales and for Scotland.

Prior to the 1974/5 reorganisation of local government, the division of the population into urban and rural components was catered for, albeit inadequately, by the existence of 'urban' and 'rural' LAAs, and the census volumes gave aggregate figures for these groups - i.e. for the 'urban' and 'rural' populations. This distinction does not exist in the current system of local government areas. In Scotland, the problem is overcome by the long-standing practice of defining 'localities' (see note 32), but in England and Wales it has resulted in the publication of a special Preliminary Report for Towns: urban and rural areas. This gives provisional figures of population present on census night in 1981 for former County Boroughs, Municipal Boroughs and Urban Districts defined, as far as practicable, by their pre-1974 boundaries. New Towns are also included, and figures are given for rural and urban components. A second edition of this publication corrected errors detected in the first.

The various preliminary reports were published within three months of census day; their provisional figures are amended, where necessary, in the county and national volumes.

(b) County Reports By far the largest single block of 1981 census material is that provided by the County Reports (for England and Wales; Regional

16

Reports for Scotland), which run to 148 volumes (two volumes - Parts 1 and 2 - for each of the 54 Counties of England and Wales, and four volumes - Vols 1 to 4 - for each of the nine Regions and three Islands Areas of Scotland) and more than 8500 pages of tables. Each report has a standard set of tables which are listed, for England and Wales, in Appendix 6 pages 62-65. The great majority of the variables in the SAS also appear in the County Reports, so that comparisons can be made between the census results for small areas, counties, regions and the country as a whole. The layout of the tables in the County Reports, however, differs from the SAS layout, mainly because the County Reports give data for several areas (all Districts, for example), whereas SAS tables contain the results for one area only. OPCS User Guide 86: 1981 Small Area Statistics/County Reports: A Guide to Comparison provides a detailed cross-reference of the two sources.

Part 1 of each report provides variables based on the 100% data. Following the three general tables, these are organised into four main groups. Tables 4-11 cover the demographic characteristics of age, sex and marital status, together with country of birth; Tables 12-16, labelled 'economic characteristics', cross-tabulate economic position and employment status with age, sex and marital status. A third, extensive section on 'housing and amenities' (Tables 17-32) covers such characteristics as occupancy type, size, tenure and amenities, which are cross-tabulated with numbers of persons and of rooms in the households. Tables 34-41 deal with 'household composition': in this case, both households of various types and population groups living in particular types of household are cross-tabulated with economic and demographic characteristics. Table 42, dealing with Welsh language ability is, of course, unique to the Welsh county reports.

Part 2 (Tables 43-51) defines a number of population and household types and cross-tabulates these with 10% characteristics such as industry, occupation, socio-economic group and social class.

In Scotland, volumes 1 and 2 of the Regional Reports replicate the tables in Parts 1 and 2 of the English County Reports, excluding those (11, 17, 19, 20, 21, 33 and 42) for which the appropriate data are not produced north of the border. Volume 3 comprises five additional tables of variables recorded only in Scotland such as the ability to speak Gaelic, the presence or absence of an 'ancillary kitchen', the type of building (detached, semi-detached, terraced, etc.) and the 'lowest floor of living accommodation and means of access'. Scottish volume 4 takes a number of population bases (present, usually resident, in private households) and household types, and gives figures not only for Regions and Districts but also for lower levels of aggregation - Civil Parishes, Wards, Electoral Divisions, Inhabited Islands, Postcode Sectors and Localities.(33)

The various New Towns Reports - two volumes each for Scotland and for England and Wales - contain the standard county report tables for those units.

In Northern Ireland, there is no direct equivalent of the County or Regional Reports. Most of the information is provided in the 'national' volumes; there is, however, a special Report for Belfast Local Government District, containing data for that area on age, sex, marital status, birth-place, religion, households, tenure, amenities, occupation density, availability of cars, communal establishments, economically active population and employment status.

17

As already indicated, the tables in the County and Regional Reports contain most of the variables available from the Small Area Statistics (though to a different format), and User Guide 86 provides a link between the two. At the same time, the County/Region table layout is extensively used in the 'national' volumes. Thus a very wide range of census variables can be examined at a great variety of spatial scales.

(c) National Volumes These include some volumes for Great Britain - but none for the United Kingdom as a whole - and others for Scotland, Northern Ireland, England and Wales or Wales only. They fall into two main types - those which replicate, usually at different levels of aggregation, the tables found in the County and Regional Reports, and those which contain additional material.

In the first category are the Scottish Summary (two volumes), the Report for Wales (which, like other volumes dealing specifically with Wales, is also published separately in Welsh), the Northern Ireland Summary Report and the two-part National Report: Great Britain. The contents of this cluster of volumes can be described in terms of the standard table numbers used in the County and Regional Reports.

The Scottish volumes reproduce Regional Report tables 1-10, 11-16, 18, 22-32, 32-41 (vol. 1) and 34-41 (vol. 2); there are no summary equivalents of the data in volumes 3 and 4 of the Regional Reports, but two additional tables (X, Y) record the various population bases. Some of the tables give data for Scotland only; others adopt lower levels of aggregation (see Appendix 5).

The Report for Wales is more straightforward, providing standard Tables 1-51 for Wales as a whole and for its constituent counties. An additional Table 52 gives population and household counts down to District level.

The Northern Ireland Summary Report gives information for Northern Ireland as a whole and for its 26 local government Districts. The topics covered are those already listed (above) for the Belfast report.

There is no equivalent summary volume for England, and the census user requiring data for all English Counties and/or Districts must assemble these from the County Reports. Data for England as a whole and for a coarser set of areal units (see Appendix 5) are, however, available from the National Report: Great Britain volumes, Part 1 containing the 100% and Part 2 the 10% variables. The tables for Great Britain are as in the County reports. Tables for which there are no Scottish data (11, 17, 19, 20, 21, 33, 42, 44) are assembled as an appendix covering England and Wales only. Summary reports produced at a later stage (the 'key statistics' volumes) are discussed below (p.23).

A second set of national volumes, often referred to as the 'census topic' volumes, provide additional information on subjects not included or only partially covered in the County/Regional reports and the summary volumes. Each topic volume contains an appendix indicating in which other volumes of the census additional tabulations covering that topic are to be found.

Counts of the 'usually resident' population calculated by the 'transfer method' (see p. 8 above) have been published for each census since 1951. In 1981, these are contained in the volume on Usual Residence: Great Britain, which gives figures for all types of census area based on administrative divisions from the District upwards.[34]

The three basic demographic characteristics are covered in Sex, Age and Marital Status: Great Britain. The statistics are similar to those in County/Regional report Table 6, but with more detail on age and marital status and a different set of areal units.

An age group of particular concern is dealt with in considerable detail in Persons of Pensionable Age: Great Britain. The usually resident population of pensionable age[35] is shown by marital status, sex and age; persons of pensionable age, by age and sex, are divided between private and non-private households and classified as residents or visitors. The tables also show changes since 1961 in the size of households containing persons of pensionable age and give the household characteristics of those households with one or more usually resident pensioners. Since many elderly people are in communal establishments, this volume also shows the number of persons of pensionable age, by broad age groups, according to the type of establishment and whether or not they are usually resident therein.

The latter aspect is taken further in the volume on Communal Establishments: Great Britain. The population, by sex, is allocated to the 'present resident', 'absent resident' and 'visitor' categories, and the age, sex and marital status of those in private and non-private households respectively are also given. Most of the additional data, as the volume title suggests, refer to those not in private households, including their 'status in the establishment' (whether staff or otherwise)[36]. For hotels and boarding houses, the tables show number of rooms and population present, with their status. 'Guests' are tabulated by age, sex and marital status and whether resident or visitors. Inmates in hospitals, homes and similar establishments are tabulated by type of establishment and the individual's economic position, whether resident or visitor and whether born within or outside the United Kingdom.

Details of the educational attainments of the population are provided by the volume on Qualified Manpower, Great Britain, in which the base population is all persons aged 18 or over and the only qualifications recorded are those normally achieved beyond that age ('A' level GCE qualifications, which were recorded in 1971, are excluded).

Three 'levels of qualification' are identified: (a) higher degrees, (b) 'first degrees or other qualifications of the standard of a first degree' and (c) 'qualifications which generally satisfy the three requirements of being (i) obtained at age 18 or over, (ii) above GCE 'A' level or SCE and (iii) below first degree level (most teaching and nursing qualifications, for example, are in category (c)).

The first three of the eleven tables in this volume identify all 'qualified persons' by level of qualification and subdivide them by age, sex, economic position and economic activity. Tables 4 and 5 give an occupational and industrial breakdown of both the total 18+ population and the qualified population at each level. Tables 6 and 7 classify the qualified at each

19

level according to the subject area in which the qualification was obtained;
Tables 8, 9, 10 and 11 cross-tabulate subject area with economic position,
employment status, occupation and industry. Most of the tables give a breakdown by age and sex, but only 1, 2 and 7 provide a regional breakdown: the
remainder give Great Britain totals only.

Data on other topics appear either in separate volumes for England and
Wales and for Scotland, or in Great Britain volumes with supplementary
information in separate Scottish publications.

Among such topics, the most complex is migration, which produces the
largest single set of census topic volumes: 24 in all. These are: National
Migration: Great Britain, Part 1 (100% tables) and Part 2 (10% tables);
Regional Migration reports - Part 1 (100%) and Part 2 (10%) - for each of
the nine Standard Regions of England and Wales; and the four Scottish
Migration volumes, Volumes 1 and 2 covering the 100% and Volumes 3 and 4 the
10% variables.

In the 100% section (part 1) of the Great Britain national migration
report, migrants[37] are first tabulated according to their origins and
destinations.[38] Migrants, by age, sex and marital status are then classified by 'type of move'[39] and (by age and sex only) by 'distance of
move';[40] adult migrants are also classified by economic position and
employment status. 'Wholly moving households' are identified by type of
move, type of household, tenure, economic position and employment status of
the head of household, amenities, availability of cars and occupation
density (persons per room). Migrants who are not part of such households
are also tabulated.

In the 10% section (Part 2) migrants, by type and distance of movement,
are classified by employment status, occupation, industry and socio-economic
group.

As already indicated, the Regional Migration reports are also divided
into 100% and 10% sections (Parts). These give much the same data as the
national reports, but to a different areal base.

The Scottish migration volumes have a somewhat different arrangement and
present variables which are similar to but not always precisely the same as
those in the volumes for Great Britain and the English regions. Volumes 1
and 3 cover the items in Parts 1 and 2 of the national report, volumes 2 and
4 are the equivalent of the English regional reports. Thus volumes 1 and 2
contain the 100% and 3 and 4 the 10% items.

International, as distinct from internal, migration[41] is treated in
the 'country of birth' volumes for Great Britain and Scotland. Country of
Birth: Great Britain comprises eight tables. Three of these give a regional
breakdown showing the country of birth of the usually resident population by
age, sex and marital status and the country of birth, and the age and sex of
residents who had entered the United Kingdom during the year prior to the
census. [42] The remaining five tables give Great Britain totals only: the
usually resident population is classified by country of birth, age, sex and
marital status; those usually resident in private households by age, sex,
whether born inside or outside the United Kingdom and by the birthplace of
the household head. Birthplaces of all heads of household are also

20

tabulated. The population not in private households is classified by type of establishment, status in the establishment, country of birth, and sex. Private households with usual residents are divided into household types and these are cross-tabulated with the birthplaces of the household heads. Finally, the population present in both 1971 and 1981 is classified by country of birth, whether a visitor to the U.K., and sex.

The Country of Birth volume for Scotland has precisely the same tables, five for Scotland as a whole and three with a regional breakdown.

Another complex set of material is covered in the volume on Housing and Households: England and Wales and the equivalent Housing and Household Report for Scotland. The England and Wales volume contains 31 tables, of which 13 give data for the country as a whole and 18 give a regional breakdown. An initial table identifies 'household spaces'[43] by type (permanent or non-permanent, self-contained, shared, etc.) and occupancy (with residents, vacant, etc.). Subsequent tables refer either to 'private households with usual residents' or to specified types of such households - households with children or with pensioners, for example. The variables presented for households include tenure, number of rooms, persons per room, amenities, availability of cars, and number of persons economically active, which are cross-tabulated in a variety of ways.

The Scottish volume contains a similar set of tables and, in addition, reproduces SAS tables 28-29, 31, 32, 41, 43 for Scotland as a whole and 10-15 at District level.

Further details on a household basis appear in the volumes on Household and Family Composition for England & Wales and Scotland respectively. These contain tables based on the structures of households and families as derived from answers to the census question (5) on 'relationship within the household'. Households are classified by type, size, number of rooms, persons per room, and numbers of wage-earners, dependent children and persons of pensionable age. Information is also given on the number and type of families, age and economic activity of the mother, type of lone parent and economic activity, social class, socio-economic group and country of birth of the head of household. Of the 34 complex tables in these volumes, only two (household size and family type) provide a regional breakdown; the rest are all for England and Wales or for Scotland as a whole.

Economic aspects are covered in detail in Economic Activity: Great Britain and the companion Scottish volume, for which the base population is all persons aged 16 or over in each area.[44] 18 tables, six of them with a regional breakdown, analyse this population by age, sex and area of workplace[45] according to its economic position,[46] employment status,[47] occupational and industrial class and socio-economic group. Supplementary tables compare the occupational structures of the population of Great Britain in 1971 and 1981. A selection of these data down to District level are provided in 64 microfiche Economic Activity Booklets, one for each Region of Scotland and County of England and Wales.

The great majority of the data mentioned so far are tabulated according to the individual's area of residence. However, as the Economic Activity volumes indicate many people work outside the area in which they reside, and home and workplace are linked in Workplace and Transport to Work volumes, of which there are two - one for Scotland and one for England and Wales. Both are based on the 10% sample.

Each volume contains a similar set of seven tables, covering the 'usually resident (economic activity) population' (i.e. persons aged 16 or over). Table 1 identifies, for each area, the numbers of people economically active or out of employment and, for those in employment, the number in each residence/workplace category - 'usually resident and working in the area', 'usually resident in the area but working outside', 'working in the area but resident outside' and the residual category 'usually resident in the area, workplace not fixed/not stated'. Tables 2 and 3 cross-tabulate the residences and workplaces of the employed population (with a fixed and stated workplace) in both directions, giving 'area of usual residence by area of workplace' and 'area of workplace by area of usual residence'. In Tables 4 and 5, the members of each residence/workplace category are sub-divided by social class, socio-economic group, occupation order and industrial class. Table 6 identifies the means of travel to work for the same three groups and Table 7 cross-tabulates (for the population in private households only) mode of travel to work with the number of cars available to the household. Data are given in each case for males, females and the total population down to the level of Districts or their equivalent (with the exception of Table 7, which gives figures for regions and counties only).

As already indicated, questions on linguistic ability in the British census are confined to those on Welsh (in Wales) and Scottish Gaelic (in Scotland). The answers to these questions form the basis of two special volumes: the Welsh Language in Wales report and the Gaelic Report for Scotland.

The data for Northern Ireland are published completely separately from those for the rest of the United Kingdom. The Preliminary and Summary reports and the special report for the Belfast local government District have already been mentioned. In addition there are five further volumes:

The Northern Ireland Economic Activity Report divides the population into 'economically active' and 'economically inactive' sections and analyses the employed population by industry and occupation, cross-tabulated with age, sex, marital status, employment status, socio-economic group, workplace and other characteristics. Most of the data are given only for the country as a whole, but in some cases there is a breakdown by District.

The Northern Ireland Workplace and Transport to Work Report gives details of the residence and workplace of the employed population. Movement to work is analysed, at District level, in relation to occupation, industry, socio-economic group, means of transport and time of journey.

The Northern Ireland Migration Report covers the numbers and charac-teristics of one-year migrants, together with their origins and destinations.

The Northern Ireland Education Report gives, for the country as a whole, the numbers, age, sex, occupation and industry of persons with 'higher educational qualifications'.

The Northern Ireland Religion Report, which is unique to that part of the U.K. provides data on the sex, age, marital status, occupation, industry and other characteristics for each of the main religious denominations.

22

The sheer scale of the published output from the 1981 census presents problems to the user requiring quick and easy access to a basic piece of information for a particular area. To aid such users, and as part of "a deliberate effort to increase the availability of the results" of the census, OPCS and GRO(S) jointly produced the valuable summary volume Key Statistics for Local Authorities, Great Britain which presents some 120 variables for the 459 local government districts of Great Britain, together with aggregates for the constituent counties, regions and countries.

The data are displayed in 19 standard tables for Scotland, Wales and each of the eight English regions. The tables themselves are organised into two groups - 'Population' and 'Households' - and within each group are arranged by topic. There are eight topics: in the 'Population' section, the 'summary' tables give both population present and the usually resident population; subsequent tables are based on the latter and cover age structure, 'social' attributes (country of birth, social class, higher education), 'work' (economic activity, industry, employment) and 'transport' (travel to work, availability of cars). The 'Households' section deals with household size, households with children and 'housing' (tenure, number of rooms, amenities).

In contrast to the other published volumes, where the data are almost universally in the form of counts, this publication gives the majority of variables as percentages of the appropriate total (which is also given),[48] thus reducing the amount of computation to be carried out by the user. In many cases, 1971-81 percentage changes are also indicated. Several of the variables are mapped, and the appendices indicate other sources - both published and SAS - for the variables appearing in this volume.

A further set of 'key statistics' volumes gives selected information for urban areas as identified for the purposes of the 1981 census, which contain some 90 per cent of the population of Great Britain. There are six volumes in this series Key Statistics for Urban Areas, Great Britain, Key Statistics for Localities (Scotland) and four regional volumes - Key Statistics for Urban Areas, the North, the Midlands, the South East and the South West and Wales[49]. The Great Britain volume gives data for 302 urban areas with populations of 20 000 or more and for 281 subdivisions of those areas; the regional and Scottish volumes cover all urban areas/ localities with 1000 or more inhabitants. Each volume contains five standard tables: (i) population, age and birthplace, (ii) social class, higher quali- fications and industry, (iii) economic activity and unemployment, (iv) house- hold tenure, amenities and cars, (v) household size and type, pensioners and children. The Great Britain volume also provides these data for urban and rural populations aggregated to the county level and for urban areas grouped by population size. Maps are provided showing the location and boundaries of each urban area.

(iii) Supplementary Documents

Attention must also be drawn to the wide range of supplementary documents produced by the census offices. The volume of such material for the 1981 census is much greater than on any previous occasion and lack of space precludes a full listing in this CATMOG. A brief summary is given below; full details may be obtained from the census offices, which produce Annual Calendars of their publications.

Mention has already been made of the OPCS Monitor series which contain selected census data - the County Monitors (CM), Ward and Civil Parish Monitors (WCPM) and Parliamentary Constituency Monitors (PCM 81, PCM 83). In addition to these, the series OPCS Monitors: Census 1981 (CEN) has been in production since 1978. Issues prior to 1981 reported on the preparations for the census; those published since the census contain a variety of material, including a note on each census publication as it appeared, details of the Small Area Statistics, explanations of the terms used in the census, reports on the Post-Enumeration Survey and comments on the census results. A list of titles is provided in Appendix 8 page 69. GRO Scotland produces a similar series of Census Information Bulletins.

A third set of OPCS Monitors draws on information from sources additional to the census. There are 23 different series on individual topics such as fertility, morbidity, mortality, migration, etc. These series are listed in Appendix 9 page 70.

User Guides, which now number around 200 and thus cannot be listed in this CATMOG, are a series of technical notes explaining the nature and layout of the census data. User Guide 52: Small Area Statistics 100% and 10%: Standard Table layouts and cell numbers is reproduced as Appendix 4, pages 50-59. User Guide 79: Change in Small Areas 1971/81; Census Tracts/Parishes and the Change Files deals with the problems of comparing 1971 and 1981 SAS and further details are given in User Guide 84: Guide to Statistical Comparability 1971-81: England and Wales (see below, Section VIII(v)).

A welcome development since the establishment of OPCS has been the publication of research reports by the staff of the census offices and others on a wide range of population topics. The quarterly journal Population Trends, now in its tenth year of publication, contains notes on data sources and a standard series of data on fertility, mortality, migration and population change, as well as short research papers. Longer research monographs appear in two series: OPCS Occasional Publications and Studies on Medical and Population Subjects.

VIII   COMPARABILITY, 1971-1981

Mention has already been made in several places in this CATMOG of the problems likely to arise when the census user attempts to compare the 1981 results with those of 1971 in order to examine the changes which occurred between the two dates. This important aspect requires more systematic treatment. Problems of comparability can arise from at least four factors, more than one of which may be applicable to a particular item or set of census data. These are:

(1)   changes in the population base
(2)   changes in the areal base
(3)   changes in the classifications used
(4)   changes in the variables presented and their arrangement in the tables.

Each of these will now be discussed in turn, together with the efforts which have been made to overcome the resultant problems. It must be realised that a 'solution' to any one of the four main problems does not necessarily imply a solution of the remaining three. References in this section will be mainly to the Small Area Statistics, but most of what is said here applies also to the data in the published volumes.

(i) Changes in the population base

Attention has already been drawn (above, p. 6) to the 1981 substitution of a 'usually resident' population base for the 'persons present' base used in earlier censuses. This change inevitably produced 1981 base populations for areal units which were not directly comparable with their 1971 and earlier equivalents. This problem can, it is true, be overcome with regard to the total population of each area. The 1981 SAS (Table 1) give 1981 figures for both the 1981 population base ('all present residents' plus 'all absent residents' = 'all residents'[50]) and the 1971 base ('all present residents' plus 'all visitors' = 'population present'). The latter can be compared with the 1971 totals, thus permitting the identification of the changes which have occurred between the two dates in the numbers of people present at the time of the census, thus continuing a procedure followed in studies of population change during earlier intercensal periods.[51] The only other section of the SAS in which both bases appear is that relating to household size ('households with x persons', Table 17).

Figures to the 1971 population base also appear occasionally in the published volumes, notably in the County Monitor series, though usually at a coarser resolution than those to the 1981 base (e.g. Counties rather than Districts).

For the great majority of the cells in the SAS, direct comparisons with the equivalent 1971 values are invalid not only because of the introduction of many new tables in 1981, but also because sub-sets such as age, sex, or marital status groups in 1981 were sub-sets of the 'usually resident' population, and in 1971 of the 'population present' on census night. In the case of the published volumes, however, comparison is valid in certain cases, notably in the 'national' volumes (see Section VII(ii)) on migration, household composition, economic activity and journey to work which, in 1971, were based on the 'usually resident' population arrived at by either the 'present/absent' or the 'transfer' system described above on pages 8-9 (Definitions, OPCS, 1981, 24).

When undertaking any comparison through time, the census user is advised to pay particular attention to the table headings and to the various descriptive guides to the census material. Variables which at first sight appear to be precisely the same in successive censuses cannot be relied upon to give precise measures of change.

(ii) Changes in the areal base

Changes of this kind are a perennial problem to the census user, even if he is concerned only with the published volumes, since it has been extremely common for the boundaries of Local Authority and other 'official' areas used in those volumes to change between successive censuses. Here too, the problem is relatively easy to overcome in the case of total population numbers, for the boundary changes are meticulously recorded in the published volumes and it has long been the practice of the census authorities to present, in the volumes relating to one census, population totals from the

preceding censuses adjusted to the new boundaries. At the level of Local
Authority Areas, this is often done for two earlier censuses;[52] the
Preliminary Report of the 1981 census of England and Wales, for example,
gives 1961 and 1971 figures adjusted to 1981 boundaries. This process was
taken much further in the case of the 1971 data, which, as reported in our
previous CATMOG (Dewdney, 1981, 21), were re-aggregated and republished for
LAAs established as a result of the local government reforms of 1974/75.
Since relatively few of the 1974/75 LAA boundaries had changed by 1981, the
areal base at this level presents only minor difficulties for most census
variables.

Local Authority Areas are subdivided into Wards, the boundaries of which
change more frequently than do those of the 'parent' LAAs. To cope with
this, OPCS has adopted a policy of continuous update whereby the 1981 basic
counts of population and households are made available for new Wards during
the year following that in which the latter are created.

The problems of a changing areal base are most severe at the level of
the census' basic territorial unit, the Enumeration District (ED). ED
boundaries inevitably change between censuses - indeed, they are completely
redesigned on each occasion - partly because of changes in the pattern of
administrative areas, but mainly owing to changes in the distribution of
population and households (see Dewdney, 1981, 8). Of the 112 280 EDs used
in the 1981 census of England and Wales, barely 50 000 were the same as those
used in 1971. At the same time, the census user concerned with intercensal
change requires a consistent set of areal units for which comparisons between
the two censuses can be made: to meet this need, new 1981 EDs were either
aggregates or subdivisions of those used in 1971 wherever this was possible
within the constraints on ED design (p.10 above).

The possibility of comparing 1971 and 1981 data has been greatly increased by the decision of OPCS to provide, for England and Wales, a large
number of variables for a set of areal units which can be identified in
terms of both 1971 and 1981 EDs: these areas are referred to as 'census
tracts'. The official guide to this set of material (OPCS, 1982)[53]
describes it as follows:

There are two main problems in making comparisons between 1971 and 1981
Census SAS. First, the local geographical base of the census changed -
to meet changed physical circumstances, to meet the reorganisation of
local government in 1974 and the subsequent revision of Ward boundaries,
to meet operational needs of the census, and to meet users' local
requirements. Second, the censuses differed in topics covered, in
question design, definitions, classifications and codings, and in the
range of local statistics required - all reflected in differences
between 1971 and 1981 SAS ... Because of the need for a systematic
approach to these problems, OPCS in England and Wales, with sponsorship
from the Department of the Environment, has identified comparable small
areas, has determined which statistics are comparable and has produced
magnetic tape files of these statistics for the comparable areas
throughout England and Wales.

The situation in Scotland is somewhat different:

26

The General Register Office (Scotland) has retabulated the 1971 census data using the 1981 SAS table outlines as far as the available data will allow. In Scotland alone it has been possible to tabulate the 1971 data for 100 per cent of usual residents, since special coding was undertaken in Scotland. The addition of unit postcodes to individual 1971 household records has permitted re-formatted figures to be available for areas built up from unit postcodes, including 1981 Enumeration Districts.

In Scotland, then, comparisons can be made at the level of 1981 EDs; in England and Wales this is possible only for the specially defined 'comparable small areas'. The design of these units differs as between former urban areas (County Boroughs, Municipal Boroughs, Urban Districts - see Dewdney, 1981, 50) and areas which were formerly Rural Districts.

In former urban areas, census tracts were defined in terms of 1971 and 1981 EDs lying within unchanged boundaries. A tract consists of either a single ED the boundaries of which had remained the same or a group of EDs the external boundaries of which were the same on both occasions. In former Rural Districts, the Civil Parishes (in Wales, the Communities) provide a suitable areal base for 1971/81 comparisons. Very few of these units have undergone boundary changes since 1971; where this has occurred, details are given. In addition, Civil Parishes with populations above 10 000 have been divided into tracts.

The 'comparable small areas' for England and Wales total 60 295 (48 336 'urban' tracts and 11 959 Civil Parishes or Communities - see Appendix 3, p.48) as compared with 109 586 EDs in 1971 and 112 280 in 1981. For Great Britain as a whole there are 78 062 comparable small areas as against 125 475 1971 EDs and 130 047 1981 EDs.[54]

The amount of comparable information which can be given for these areas is, however, somewhat limited. Only 100% variables are treated. There were:

840 counts in the 100% 1971 SAS and some 3000 counts in the corresponding parts of the 1981 SAS. After excluding counts that cannot be compared and excluding some further counts where comparison is possible but of doubtful validity, there are 452 that are common to both sets and can reasonably be compared. Only 103 counts are strictly comparable: the major qualification affecting the remainder is the change in the base population counted. (Morgan and Denham, 1982)

OPCS produce, for each 'comparable small area', a standard set of 22 'change-file tables', containing 479 variables giving comparable data from the two censuses (see Section VIII(v) below). Transparent overlays of Ordnance Survey 1:10 000 map sheets, showing the boundaries of census tracts are also available.

Dissatisfaction with LAAs and other 'official' areas as a basis for the presentation of census data has prompted a number of research workers to devise their own sets of territorial units. Prominent among these has been the team at the Centre for Urban and Regional Development Studies (CURDS), University of Newcastle upon Tyne, who have succeeded in "identifying a set of centres on the basis of their importance for employment and shopping and then allocating the areas between these centres to the places with which

27

they are most closely linked in terms of journey-to-work movements". This has been done on the basis of pre-1974 LAAs, or subdivisions of them to which data from 1971 and 1981 SAS can be aggregated. The result is a set of 228 'Functional Regions' which are further subdivided into 'Cores' (the cities' main built-up areas), 'Rings' (the primary commuting hinterlands), 'Outer Areas' (secondary commuting hinterlands) and 'Rural Areas' (relatively self-contained areas without large urban centres of their own, but looking towards the cities for high-level services). This produces a total of 627 'Zones' which together cover the entire surface of Great Britain (see CURDS, 1983-4; Champion, Coombes and Openshaw, 1984).

An outstanding innovation of the 1971 census was the publication of the full range of Small Area Statistics re-aggregated to 100 m (in some areas), 1 km, 10 km and 100 km squares of the National Grid (Dewdney, 1981, 14). Mainly for reasons of economy, this procedure was not repeated in 1981. However, 'grid square' data from the 1981 census are provided in a different way. 100 metre grid references are allocated to ED centroids and the data for each ED can thus be allocated to the appropriate grid square. The resultant figures are approximations rather than the precise grid-square statistics produced in 1971. Data in this form have been used by OPCS in the production of their People in Britain wall-chart series, where the value for each grid square is represented by a coloured dot.

(iii) Changes in the classifications used

Certain of the categories tabulated in 1981 - 'households with heads born in the New Commonwealth or Pakistan', for example - were not used in 1971. Conversely, some of the items recorded in 1971, for instance certain household amenities, were dropped in 1981. In cases such as these, obviously, no comparisons can be made. Elsewhere, the 1981 classification is more detailed, as with marital status or mode of transport to work: here, provided that the problems described in VIII(i) and (ii) above can be solved, it is a simple matter to aggregate the 1981 data to 1971 categories.

The matter becomes slightly more complex in cases where social change has affected the categories used. Age structure provides an illustration. In 1972, the legal school-leaving age in the United Kingdom was raised from 15 to 16 years. Thus the category 'children' was defined in 1971 as 'any person less than 15' and in 1981 as 'any person less than 16' years of age. Adults were persons aged 15 or over in 1971, 16 or over in 1981. (The minimum legal age of marriage, however, was 16 on both occasions). Such changes indicate the need for care in the use of variables relating to children or adults.

They have also affected the layout of the age-structure tables. Since five-year age groups, or aggregates of these such as 0-14, 15-64, 65+, are commonly used in international comparisons and in studies of changes in the population's age structure through time, it must still be possible to derive these from the census data. Consequently, British census tables showing five-year age groups (e.g. SAS Table 2) tabulate 15 year-olds separately so that these can be added to the 0-14 year-olds (thus identifying all 'children') or to the 16-19 year-olds (producing the 15-19 five-year group) as required by the census user. Another aspect of age structure concerns the 'persons of pensionable age' who are identified in many census tables. These are men aged 65 or over and women aged 60 or over. Thus age and sex data must be aggregated in at least two different ways, one giving standard age groups, the other giving such classes as 'adults below pensionable age' and 'pensionable adults', the age bounds of which are different for each sex. Once again, the census user must exercise care in the selection of variables for study.

The problem of changes in the categories used is greatest in the more complex classifications, notably those of industry, occupation, socio-economic group and social class, the latter pair depending primarily on the former. Classifications of the population according to the industries in which it works have been a standard feature of British censuses since 1921, and are based on the Standard Industrial Classification (SIC) used by the Department of Employment and its predecessors. This has been changed on several occasions and the 1951, 1961, 1971 and 1981 censuses used SICs drawn up in 1948, 1958, 1968 and 1980 respectively. As regards occupation, prior to 1972, "the classification of occupations prepared by OPCS primarily for census purposes was the sole list used within government for the statistical study of occupations" (Boston, 1980). In 1972, the Department of Employment produced a Classification of Occupations and Dictionary of Occupational Titles (CODOT), which was used for the 1981 census.

In both these cases, considerable effort, involving close study of the classifications themselves and of the explanatory documents produced by the census offices is necessary in order to extract comparable groups from the 1971 and 1981 census data.

The division of the population into 'socio-economic groups' and social classes is carried out in the census offices on the basis of answers to the questions on economic activity, employment status, occupation and industry. Although the titles used in these classifications were the same in 1981 as they had been in 1971, there is no guarantee that exactly the same categories of people were allocated to them. Boston (1980), for example, quotes cases of occupational groups which were assigned to different social classes in the two censuses.

Finally, it must be emphasised that care should always be taken to note the age groups to which these classifications apply. Many of the variables presented for occupation, industry, socio-economic group and social class refer to adults only, that is to persons aged 15 or over in 1971, 16 or over in 1981.

(iv) Changes in the variables presented and their arrangement in tables

The fourth of our sources of difficulty, which arises mainly from the great increase in the output of census data, requires no further discussion. Changes in census output become apparent if we compare the details given in Section VII above and in Appendices 4, 5 and 7 with the equivalent sections of our earlier CATMOG (Dewdney, 1981, 14-22, 33-42).

(v) OPCS User Guide 84

Discussions of the problems involved in comparing 1971 and 1981 census material and information on how this can best be done appear in a variety of census office publications. Following the production of the full range of census data, much of this material was consolidated in OPCS User Guide 84:

29

Guide to Statistical Comparability 1971-81: England and Wales, which consti-
tutes an essential source of information for census users intending to make
comparisons between the 1971 and 1981 data. Although the guide deals mainly
with comparisons between the Small Area Statistics from the two censuses,
much of what it contains is relevant to users of the published volumes and
other types of census output.

Following a general statement of the problems involved, User Guide 84
lists the topic content of the two censuses according to the question numbers
on the schedules. This is followed by a discussion of "who and what was
counted" and the various data-processing procedures used by the census
offices.

The reader is then introduced to the 'change files', which contain all
those variables for which comparable figures can be produced from the two
censuses. These 'change file variables' are arranged in a standard set of
Change File Tables, which are reproduced in this CATMOG as Appendix 11. The
guide then lists the table and cell numbers of the change files and cross-
references these to the equivalent table and cell numbers in the 1971 and
1981 SAS, (The '1971-81 change-file listing of comparable cells').

IX POST-CENSUS CHECKS

Work in connection with a particular census by no means comes to an end once
the results of that census have been collected, processed and published.
The census offices carry out post-census checks of various kinds with a view
to assessing the accuracy of the census and as a guide to those aspects of
the process which might be improved on future occasions.[55]

The most important of these was the 'Post-Enumeration Survey' (PES),
carried out by the Social Survey Division of OPCS between April and June
1981 in a sample of just over 1000 Enumeration Districts. This included a
check on the original Enumerators' listings of households and, at households
where no-one was present on census night, a check to see if any individuals
had been entirely omitted from the census. In addition, the quality of the
answers in the census schedules was checked by detailed interviews with a
sample of about 5000 private households. The PES thus included both a
'coverage check' and a 'quality check'.

From the coverage check, it has been estimated that about 296 000 people
present in private households in England and Wales on census night (0.62% of
the total) were omitted from the census. This error was distributed among a
variety of causes as shown in Table 1.

In addition, an estimated 83 000 persons were double-counted giving a
net under-enumeration of 214 000 or 0.45%. Both under-enumeration and double
counting were most common among the more mobile sections of the population,
particularly young adults and especially the unemployed and students. Males
were 'missed' more often than females. Households missed tended to be con-
centrated in the private (especially the furnished) rented sector - the type
of accommodation most likely to be occupied by mobile young adults.

Table 1. Causes of omission of individuals from the census.

Source of error	Persons	
	000	%
Households misclassified as absent by the Enumerator	81	0.17
Household spaces misclassified as vacant by the Enumerator	41	0.09
Property missed	25	0.05
Persons missed in enumerated households	128	0.27
Other causes	21	0.04
Gross under-enumeration	296	0.62

The net under-enumeration of 214 000 (0.45 per cent) was unevenly distributed among the various types of area. An estimated 58 000 persons (2.46%) were 'missed' in Inner London and 42 000 (1.01%) in Outer London, but only 27 000 (0.24%) in other metropolitan areas and 87 000 (0.29%) in the rest of the country.

Finally, it may be noted that, towards the end of 1983 it was announced that the idea of a mid-term census in 1986 had been rejected, mainly on economic grounds,[56] and that planning in the census offices will proceed on the assumption that the next census will take place in April 1991.

NOTES

1. The census offices are
   - for England and Wales: the Office of Population Censuses and Surveys, St. Catherine's House, 10 Kingsway, London WC2B 6JP;
   - for Scotland: the Census Office, General Register Office (Scotland), Ladywell House, Ladywell Road, Edinburgh EH12 7TF;
   - for Northern Ireland: the Census Office, Department of Finance, Management Services Building, 11 Stoney Road, Stormont, Belfast BT4 3UP.

2. The Preliminary Report (q.v.) gives the following population counts for 1981:

	000	%
England	46 221	82.73
Wales	2 790	4.99
England and Wales	49 011	87.72
Scotland	5 117	9.16
Great Britain	54 129	96.88
Northern Ireland	1 547	2.77
United Kingdom	55 676	99.65
Isle of Man	62	0.11
Channel Islands	133	0.24
Total	55 870	100.00

3. There were separate questionnaires for England, Scotland, Wales and Northern Ireland. This was the procedure also adopted in 1971, but on previous occasions there had been separate 100% and 10% questionnaires (see Dewdney, 1981, 9).

4. This set of questions was "not very satisfactorily answered in 1971" and OPCS hoped "to analyse fertility on somewhat similar lines to previous censuses by using information from the 1981 census about children shown as part of a family" (OPCS, 1977).

5. OPCS Monitors: Census 1981, listed in Appendix 8 p.69.

6. Census 1981: Census Topics, listed in Appendix 10 p.70.

7. The last volume of 1971 results was not published until 1978. Publication of the full set of 1981 results was achieved, on schedule, during 1984.

8. This applies to England and Wales: Scottish enumerators did not pre-list households and the publicity leaflet was delivered with the census schedule.

   The procedures for defining and identifying 'buildings' and 'dwellings' were somewhat different from those used in 1971 (for details, see Definitions, OPCS, 1981) and the concept of the 'household' as the basic unit of enumeration was slightly modified. A household is defined for census purposes as "either one person living alone or a group of people (who may or may not be related) living, or staying temporarily, at the same address with common housekeeping. Enumerators were to treat a group of people as a household if there was any regular arrangement to share at least one meal a day, breakfast counting as a meal, or if the occupants shared a common living or sitting room". The last phrase was a new one, used for the first time in 1981.

   Communal establishments - the term now preferred to such earlier ones as 'non-private' or 'institutional' households - were separately identified.

9. There were different schedules for private households in England, Wales, Scotland and Northern Ireland; there were also 'individual' forms for persons in communal establishments and for those in private households who wished to have their own forms.

10. A full listing of the 1971 questions appears in Dewdney, 1981, Appendix 1, pages 29-32.

11. British censuses have traditionally produced some data on a 100% basis (i.e. all individuals in the appropriate category) and some on a 10% basis (i.e. from a sample of one in ten of the census schedules (see Dewdney, 1981, 12, 15).

12. In 1971, the answers to this question were used mainly to distinguish 'part-time' from 'full-time' workers, the latter being those working more than 30 hours per week. In 1981, respondents were instructed to classify themselves as part-time or full-time, again using 30 hours as the dividing line.

13. Among the topics recommended by the United Nations for inclusion in the modern census (U.N., 1967) are citizenship, national and/or ethnic group, language and religion. The British census covers none of these in a systematic, comprehensive manner. (It does, however, include all other recommended topics).

14. In the published data, however, there are attempts to locate ethnic minorities, as in the tabulations of 'residents in private households with a household head born in the New Commonwealth or Pakistan'.

15. On previous occasions, more than 70 per cent of the population of Northern Ireland answered this question.

16. The term "Head of Household" as used in the census tables is defined by OPCS as "the person entered in the first column of the schedule, provided that person was (a) aged 16 years or over and (b) usually resident at that address. If one of these conditions was not met, the first person aged 16 years or over to be entered on the schedule and recorded as usually resident at that address was to be classified as the Head. In the last resort, the oldest resident under 16 years of age would be taken as Head. No Head was identified in households consisting entirely of visitors." (Definitions, OPCS, 1981).

    This definition is recorded here as an example of the care and detail with which it is necessary to identify categories used in the census if these are to be applied consistently.

17. Persons joining the household on the day following census night who had not already been included on a census schedule filled in elsewhere were also included.

18. Modified, that is, in the sense that it was based on 'usual address' rather than on legal residence. The latter would have been very difficult, if not impossible to establish in the majority of cases.

19. Where the postcode was incomplete or not provided, it was added by OPCS using the postcode directories which link unit postcodes to the Ward, District and County in which the postcode area is wholly or mainly situated.

20. In Scotland, however, EDs do not aggregate to wards; the equivalent units - Regional Electoral Districts and Electoral District Wards (see Appendix 3) are produced by aggregating postcode areas.

21. As an example, the author's derived variable HCV (household composition variable) 279, labelled LNPNHH and defined as "Lone-pensioner households: private households with one resident of pensionable age and no other residents, per 10 000 private households", may be calculated as follows:

$$10\ 000 \times \frac{2508 + 2509 + 2510 + 2511}{929}$$

(Cells 2508-2511 are in table 32, 929 is in table 10, but it is not necessary to specify the table number since, in contrast to 1971, every cell number is unique - a welcome improvement). The 1981 SAS, in contrast to the 1971 version which inc luded a selection of ratio variables, are wholly confined to numerical counts of persons and households.

22. For the distinction between 100% and 10% variables, see p.15 of this CATMOG.

23. The layout is not wholly consistent in this respect. In Table 11, for example, there is no cell number for 'total household spaces in hotels and boarding houses', marked xxx.

24. In contrast to the published volumes on migration (q.v.), the SAS give no information on the direction of movement. The 1981 SAS are less detailed than 1971 in failing to distinguish between 'migrants within' and 'migrants into' the LAA.

25. For the definition of 'household', see Note 8, above.

26. The 'errors' occur if the 10% sample for an ED is assumed to be fully representative of the population, i.e. if we assume that a 10% figure multiplied by ten gives the 'real' total. The 10% figures are, of course, as accurate as any others in the census in stating that the 10% of schedules included in the sample produced a certain number of persons in a particular category.

27. For their addresses, see Note 1, above.

28. The various Census Monitor pamphlet series and their equivalents are not included in these totals.

29. Local Authority Areas in 1971 were: in England and Wales 1425 (59 Counties, 84 County Boroughs, 32 London Boroughs, 259 Municipal Boroughs, 522 Urban Districts, 469 Rural Districts); in Scotland 432 (33 Counties, 4 Cities, 21 Large Burghs, 176 Small Burghs, 198 Districts).

    Local Authority Areas in 1981 were: in England and Wales 453 (7 Metropolitan Counties, 47 Non-metropolitan Counties, 33 London Boroughs, 366 Districts); in Scotland 65 (9 Regions, 3 Island Areas, 53 Districts).

30. There was no 1981 equivalent of the 1971 Advance Analysis volumes for England and Wales or the Great Britain Summary 1% Sample) tables.

31. This applies in England and Wales; in Scotland a selection of material at Ward, Civil Parish and Postcode sector levels is included in the Regional Reports.

32. Even before the reorganisation of Scottish local government in 1975, there had been a long-standing problem regarding the division between urban and rural areas. Administrative boundaries defined only cities, burghs and districts, but many sizeable urban areas were never accorded burgh status. Consequently, the census publications also record the population of 'localities', defined for 1981 as "continuously built-up areas with populations of 500 or more in 1971".

33. The units used differ between the various tables - not every type of area appears in every table. The information given here is similar to but not identical with that in the Ward and Civil Parish Monitors for England and Wales.

34. These figures were used as a base for the Registrar-General's revised mid-1981 population estimates from which later annual estimates were calculated.

35. Women 60+, Men 65+.

36. This provides another example of the need for a careful definition of terms. Classifications of communal establishments and the people in them are given in Definitions (OPCS, 1981), 10-11.

37. In all cases, 'migrants' are one-year migrants only, i.e. those whose usual address one year ago was different from the usual address at the time of the census.

38. That is their 'usual address one year ago' and 'usual address at the time of the census'.

39. 'Type of move' distinguishes between movements within and movements between the areas specified.

40. 'Distance of move' is a new feature of the 1981 census. Migrants are classified according to the distance between the usual address one year ago and the usual address at the time of the census. The distance classes are 0-4, 5-9, 10-19, 20-49, 50-79 and 80 or more kilometres.

41. In this case, the migrants are, of course, 'lifetime migrants', persons who, at the time of the census were found in a country other than that in which they had been born.

42. Here, one-year international migrants are identified.

43. 'Household spaces' are the units of accommodation identified by the Enumerator. Not all of these necessarily contained 'residents' at the time of the census: some were 'vacant', some contained 'visitors' but no persons 'usually resident' there.

44. Referred to throughout as the 'usually resident (economic activity) population'.

45. Whether within or outside the area of residence.

46. 'Economic position' categories include: persons in employment (full-time or part-time) and persons out of employment (temporarily sick, other reasons).

47. 'Employment status' categories are: self-employed (with or without employees), employees (managers, foremen and supervisors, professional, apprentices, etc., others).

48. A procedure adopted elsewhere in 1981, for example in the County Monitor series.

49. These areas are groups of Standard Regions.

50. But note the qualifications recorded on pages 8-9 of this CATMOG

51. Provided, of course that the problems resulting from changes in the areal base can be overcome. Mounsey (1981) discusses this problem at length and has reconstructed the population present for the post-1974 counties and districts of Great Britain for all censuses since 1901. Her figures are reproduced on pages 351-364 of the Census User's Handbook (Rhind, 1983).

52. It is interesting, historically, to note that this was impossible for many areas in 1951, since the 1931 records had been destroyed by fire in 1941.

53. This is one of a large set of User Guides to the 1981 census material which can be obtained from the census offices.

54. In Scotland, 1971/81 comparisons can be made at both postcode sector and District levels as a result of the re-formatting of 1971 100% and 10% SAS.

55. Results and comments appear in the OPCS Monitor Census 1981 series, which continues to be published more than three years after census date and also lists census publications as these are made available.

56. The same fate befell a proposed 1976 census, leaving the 1966 sample census as the only British census outside the normal decennial series. The latter now comprises a run of 17 censuses (none was held in 1941). Details of the coverage of all seventeen may be obtained from Hakim (1982) and from the OPCS pamphlet Census Topics 1801-1981 (CE 30, OPCS, 3/80) published in June 1980.

REFERENCES

Boston, G. (1980). Classification of occupations. *Population Trends* 20, 9-11.

Champion, T., Coombes, M. & Openshaw, S. (1984). New regions for a new Britain. *Geographical Magazine* 56(4), 187-190.

CURDS (1983-4). *Functional Regions: Factsheets.* Centre for Urban and Regional Development Studies, University of Newcastle upon Tyne.

Denham, C. (1980). The geography of the census. 1971 and 1981, *Population Trends* 19, 6-12.

Dewdney, J.C. (1981). *The British Census.* CATMOG 29, Geo Abstracts, Norwich.

Hakim, C. (1982). *Secondary Analysis in Social Research: A guide to data sources and methods with examples.* Allen & Unwin, London.

Hansard, (1980). House of Lords April 22: cols 729-756; May 6 cols 1596-1598; House of Commons April 29, cols 1301-1337.

Morgan, C. & Denham, C. (1982). Census small area statistics (SAS): measuring change and spatial variation. *Population Trends* 28, 12-17.

Mounsey, H. (1982). The cartography of time-changing phenomena: the animated map. *Unpublished Ph.D. thesis*, University of Durham.

OPCS (1977). Planning for the 1981 Census of Population. *Population Trends* 10, 7-9.

OPCS (1978). *OPCS Monitor 1981 Census* 78/5, 2-7.

OPCS (1981). *Census 1981: Definitions, Great Britain*. (CEN 81 DEF), HMSO, London.

OPCS (1982a). Changes in small areas 1971/81; census tracts/parishes and the change files: prospectus. *OPCS Census 1981 User Guide 79*.

OPCS (1982b). 1981 Small Area Statistics/County Reports. A guide to comparison. *OPCS Census 1981 User Guide 86*.

OPCS (1984). Guide to statistical comparability 1971-81, England and Wales. *OPCS Census 1981 User Guide 84*.

Rhind, D.W. (ed.) (1983). *A Census User's Handbook*. Methuen, London.

Sillitoe, K. (1978a). Ethnic origins 1: an experiment in the use of a direct question about ethnicity for the census. *OPCS Occasional Paper* 8.

Sillitoe, K. (1978b). Ethnic origins 2, *OPCS Occasional Paper* 9.

Sillitoe, K. (1978c). Ethnic origins 3, *OPCS Occasional Paper* 10.

UN (1967). *Principles and Recommendations for the 1970 Population Censuses*, UN Statistical Papers, Series M, No. 44.

(i) The questions listed below constitute the schedule administered to private households in England

(ii) An asterisk * indicates that there was a difference between the question asked in England and its equivalent in Scotland, Wales or Northern Ireland. These differences are listed under the appropriate country in Appendix 2

(iii) Each item below is followed by a note, prefixed *71/81*, which indicates the equivalent question in 1971 and any differences between the 1971 and 1981 questions. (For precise details of the 1971 questions, see CATMOG 29 (pp.29-32))

TO BE COMPLETED BY THE ENUMERATOR

Census District, Enumeration District, Form Number, Name, Address, Postcode

(71/81: in 1971, a six-figure grid reference was also required)

*PANEL A: TO BE COMPLETED BY THE ENUMERATOR AND AMENDED, IF NECESSARY, BY THE PERSON(S) SIGNING THIS FORM

This household's accommodation is:

In a caravan	☐20
In any other mobile or temporary structure	☐30
In a purpose-built block of flats or maisonettes	☐12
In any other permanent building in which the entrance from outside the building is:	
Not shared with another household	☐10
Shared with another household	☐11

(71/81: in 1971, some of this information was supplied by answers to question A2; 1981 clarifies the distinction between households sharing/not sharing dwelling and provides additional information on the nature of the dwelling)

QUESTIONS RELATING TO THE HOUSEHOLD'S ACCOMMODATION

(71/81: the method of defining a household was slightly modified in 1981; see p.32 of this CATMOG)

*H1 Rooms. Please count the rooms in your household's accommodation. Do not count: small kitchens, that is those under 2 metres (6ft 6ins) wide, bathrooms, W.C.s. Rooms divided by curtains or portable screens count as one; those divided by a fixed or sliding partition count as two. Rooms used solely for business, professions or trade purposes should be excluded

    Number of rooms ...

(71/81: As 1971 Qn A3, with minor modification to definition of rooms to be included)

APPENDIX 1 (cont.)

*H2 Tenure. How do you and your household occupy your accommodation?

As owner occupier (including purchase by mortgage)
1☐ of freehold property
2☐ of leasehold property
By renting, rent free or by lease
3☐ from a local authority (council or New Town)
4☐ with a job, shop, farm or other business
5☐ from a housing association or charitable trust
6☐ furnished from a private landlord, company or other
    organisation
7☐ unfurnished from a private landlord, company or
    other organisation
In some other way
    please give details ....

*(71/81: As 1971 Qn A1, with the addition of the freehold/leasehold division
of owner-occupied property and of category 4 in the rented sector)*

*H3 Amenities. Has your household the use of the following amenities?
A fixed bath or shower permanently connected to a water supply and a waste
pipe.
A flush toilet (W.C.) with entrance inside the building
A flush toilet (W.C.) with entrance outside the building
In each case, the following tick boxes are provided
1☐ Yes - for use only by this household
2☐ Yes - for use also by another household
3☐ No

*(71/81: 1971 Qn A5; in 1981 the range of amenities covered is reduced from
six to three by the omission of: cooker or cooking stove; kitchen sink
permanently connected; hot water supply from heating appliance or boiler)*

H4. Answer this question if box 11 in Panel A is ticked
Are your rooms (not counting a bathroom or W.C.) enclosed behind your own
front door inside the building?
1☐ Yes   2☐ No

(71/81: equivalent of 1971 Qn A2 but reworded in 1981)

H5 Cars and vans. Please tick the appropriate box to indicate the number
of cars and vans normally available for use by you or members of your
household (other than visitors). Include any car or van provided by
employers if normally available for use by you or members of your household
but exclude vans used solely for the carriage of goods.

0☐ None;   1☐ One;   2☐ Two;   3☐ Three or more

(71/81: 1971 Qn A4 asked for precise number in all cases)

39

QUESTIONS RELATING TO INDIVIDUALS

These questions to be answered for:
- all the persons who spend Census night 5-6 April 1981 in this household (including anyone visiting overnight and anyone who arrives here on the Monday and who has not been included as present on another census form)
- any persons who usually live with your household but who are absent on census night (for example on holiday, in hospital, at school or college. Include them even if you know they are being put on another form elsewhere).

(71/81: no basic change, but in 1971 there was a separate section of the schedule (part C) with a limited range of questions to be answered for persons usually resident in the household but not present on census night. The 1981 version permits tabulation by 'usual residence')

1. Name and surname

(71/81: 1971 Qn B1 unchanged)

2. Sex ☐ Male ☐ Female

(71/81: 1971 Qn B3; in 1981 tick-boxes replace insertion of 'M' or 'F')

3. Date of Birth (day, month, year)

(71/81: 1971 Qn B2 unchanged)

*4. Marital status. Please tick the box showing the present marital status. (If separated but not divorced please tick 'Married (1st marriage)' or 'Re-married' as appropriate)

1☐ Single
2☐ Married (1st marriage)
3☐ Re-married
4☐ Divorced
5☐ Widowed

(71/81: 1971 Qn B6. In 1981, tick boxes replace insertion of marital status; categories expanded from four to five by distinction between '1st marriage' and 'Re-married')

5. Relationship in household. Please tick the box which indicates the relationship of each person to the person entered in the first column. (Please write in relationship of 'Other relative' - for example, father, daughter-in-law, brother-in-law, niece, uncle, cousin, grandchild. Please write in position in household of 'Unrelated person' - for example, boarder, housekeeper, friend, flatmate, foster-child)

01☐ Husband or wife; 02☐ Son or daughter; ☐ other relative, please specify ....; ☐ unrelated, please specify ....

(71/81: 1971 Qn B5. The 1981 question removes the concept of 'head of household', introduces tick-boxes, gives additional guidance on 'other relative' and 'unrelated')

6. __Whereabouts on night of 5-6 April 1981.__ Please tick the appropriate box to indicate where the person was on the night of 5-6 April 1981.

    1⬜At this address, out on night work or travelling to this address
    2⬜Elsewhere in England, Wales or Scotland
    3⬜Outside Great Britain

(71/81: No clear equivalent in 1971)

7. __Usual address.__ If the person usually lives here, please tick 'this address'. If not, tick 'elsewhere' and write in the person's usual address. (The home address should be taken as the usual address for a head of household who lives away from home for part of the week. For students and children away from home during term time, the home address should be taken as the usual address. Boarders should be asked what they consider to be their usual address.)

    1⬜This address
    2⬜Elsewhere - write the person's usual address and postcode ....

(71/81: 1971 Qn B4. The 1981 question attempts a clearer definition of 'usual address'. Note the occurrence of 'head of household' in this question)

8. __Usual address one year ago.__ If the person's usual address one year ago, on 5 April 1980, was the same as that given in answer to question 7 please tick box 1 'Same'. If not, please tick box 2 'Different' and write in the usual address. (For a child born since 5 April 1980 write 'Under One'.)

    1⬜Same as question 7
    2⬜Elsewhere - write the person's address and postcode on 5 April 1980 ....

(71/81: 1971 Qn B11 reworded. Note the absence of any equivalent of 1971 B12 'Usual address five years ago')

9. __Country of birth.__ Please tick the appropriate box. (If box 6 'Elsewhere' is ticked, please write in the present name of the country in which the birthplace is now situated.)

1⬜England;   2⬜Wales;   3⬜Scotland;   4⬜Northern Ireland; 5⬜Irish Republic;   6⬜Elsewhere - please write the present name of the country ....

(71/81: 1971 Qn B9 reworded. 'Date of entering U.K.', asked in 1971 is not asked in 1981. Note also the omission of 1971 Qn B10 asking the country of birth of the individual's parents)

QUESTIONS TO WHICH ANSWERS ARE NOT REQUIRED FOR PERSONS UNDER
16 YEARS OF AGE (born after 5 April 1965

*(71/81: in 1971 the equivalent questions were asked of all persons over
15, then the school leaving age)*

10. Whether working, retired, housewife, etc. last week. Please tick all
boxes appropriate to the person's activity last week. (A job (box 1 and
box 2) means any type of work for pay or profit but not unpaid work. It
includes: casual or temporary work; work on a person's own account; work in
a family business; part-time work even if only for a few hours. A part-time
job (box 2) is a job in which the hours worked, excluding any overtime, are
usually 30 hours or less per week. Tick box 1 or box 2, as appropriate, if
the person had a job but was not at work for all or part of the week
because he or she was: on holiday; temporarily laid off; on strike; sick.
For a full-time student, tick box 9 as well as any other appropriate boxes.)

1☐ In a full-time job at any time last week
2☐ In a part-time job at any time last week
3☐ Waiting to take up a job already accepted
4☐ Seeking work
5☐ Prevented by temporary sickness from seeking work
6☐ Permanently sick or disabled
7☐ Housewife
8☐ Wholly retired from employment
9☐ At school or a full-time student at an educational
     establishment not provided by an employer
0☐ Other, please specify ....

*(71/81: 1971 Qns B7 and B8 provide the nearest equivalent; the 1981
question has a larger number of categories. 1971 Qn B19 'Hours worked' is
not repeated; 1981 uses 30 hours to distinguish 'full-time' from 'part-time')*

Questions about present or previous employment

For persons in a job last week, please answer questions 11-15 in respect of
the main job during the week.
For persons wholly retired; persons out of work last week; persons prevented
from working because of permanent sickness or disablement, please answer
questions 11-13 in respect of the most recent full-time job.
For other persons, including those with no previous job, please write 'not
applicable' at question 11 and leave questions 12-15 blank.

11. Name and business of employer (if self-employed, the name and
nature of the person's business)
(a) Please give the name of the person's employer. Give the trading name
if one is used and avoid using abbreviations or initials.
Name of employer ....
(b) Please describe clearly what the employer (or the person if self-
employed) makes or does
Nature of business ....
(For a person employed in private domestic service, write 'Domestic service')

(71/81: 1971 Qn B15 reworded)

12. Occupation. (a) Please give full and precise details of the person's occupation. If a person's job is known in the trade or industry by a special name, use that name. Precise terms should be used, for example 'radio-mechanic', 'jig and tool fitter', 'tool room foreman', rather than general terms such as 'mechanic', 'fitter', 'foreman'.
Occupation ....
(b) Please describe the actual work done
Description of work ....

(71/81: 1971 Qn B16 reworded)

13. Employment status. Please tick the appropriate box. (Box 3 should be ticked for a person having management or supervisory responsibility for other employees. For a person employed as a quality control inspector and concerned only with the technical quality of a product, tick box 2.)

1☐ Apprentice or articled trainee
2☐ Employee not supervising other employees
3☐ Employee supervising other employees
4☐ Self-employed not employing others
5☐ Self-employed employing others

(71/81: 1971 Qns B17 and B18 are here combined in a single question to be answered by tick-box only. Fine distinctions in the 'apprentice or articled trainee' category asked for in 1971 Qn B18 are abandoned, but 'employee' (1971 Qn B17) is now subdivided into 'supervising/not supervising other employees')

14. Address of place of work. Please give the full address of the person's place of work. (For a person employed on a site for a long period, give the address of the site. For a person not working regularly at one place who reports daily to a depot or other fixed address, give that address.)

Full address and postcode of workplace ....
1☐ No fixed place
2☐ Mainly at home

(71/81: 1971 Qn B20 reworded)

*15. Daily journey to work. Please tick the appropriate box to show how the longest part, by distance, of the person's daily journey to work is normally made. (For a person using different means of transport on different days, show the means most often used.)

1☐ British Rail train
2☐ Underground, tube, metro, etc.
3☐ Bus, minibus or coach (public or private)
4☐ Motor cycle, scooter, moped
5☐ Car or van - pool, sharing driving
6☐ Car or van - driver
7☐ Car or van - passenger
8☐ Pedal cycle
9☐ On foot
0☐ Other; please specify ....
0☐ Works mainly at home

APPENDIX 1 (cont.)

(71/81: 1971 Qn B21 write-in replaced by tick-boxes. Categories increased by 1981 subdivision of 'rail' (1, 2) and 'car' (5, 6, 7))

QUESTION TO BE ANSWERED FOR ALL PERSONS AGED 18 OR OVER (BORN BEFORE 6 APRIL 1963)

16. Degrees, professional and vocational qualifications. Has the person obtained any qualifications after the age of 18, such as: Degrees, Diplomas, HNC, HND; Nursing qualifications, Teaching qualifications; Graduate or corporate membership of professional institutions; other professional, vocational or educational qualifications? (Exclude qualifications normally obtained at school, such as GCE, CSE and School Certificates.)

      1☐ No - none of these
      2☐ Yes - give details
      Title ....; Subjects(s) ....; Year ....;
      Institution ....

(71/81: 1971 Qn B14. 1981 question includes retired persons over 70 who were not required to answer in 1971)

(Fertility. 1971 Qns B23, B24 to be answered by married, widowed or divorced women below the age of 60, are not repeated in 1981)

44

APPENDIX 2: CENSUS SCHEDULES, 1981 FOR SCOTLAND, WALES AND NORTHERN IRELAND, WHERE DIFFERENT FROM ENGLAND

1. SCOTLAND

TO BE COMPLETED BY THE ENUMERATOR AND AMENDED, IF NECESSARY, BY THE PERSON(S) SIGNING THIS FORM

(a) Enumeration District No., Form No.; (b) Name; (c) Address, Postcode;
(d) Type of building in which household's accommodation is situated: House
that is: 1☐detached; 2☐semi-detached; 3☐terraced; Flat or
rooms in a building with: 4☐2 storeys; 5☐3 or 4 storeys;
6☐5 storeys or over; 7☐a single flat with a shop, office or other
business; Non-permanent structure: 8☐caravan; 9☐other non-
permanent structure; (e) Level of household's accommodation: (1)☐all
on ground or on ground and other floors; (2)☐all in basement;
(3)☐all on first or higher floor (state actual floor of entry ☐);
(f) Means of access to household's accommodation: 1☐no lift; no external
or internal stair (with 6 or more steps); 2☐external stair or outside
steps (with 6 or more steps); 3☐internal stair (with 6 or more steps);
4☐lift.

QUESTIONS RELATING TO THE HOUSEHOLD'S ACCOMMODATION

Rooms (a) How many rooms in your household's accommodation are dining rooms,
living rooms or bedrooms? Count spare rooms if they could be used for these
purposes .... room(s).
(b) Is cooking generally done in one of the rooms entered in (a) above?
☐Yes   ☐No
(c) Have you any room used for cooking but not included in (a) above?
☐Yes   ☐No

Tenure As England, but no freehold/leasehold division of owner-occupied
property.

Amenities W.C. with entrance inside the dwelling.

QUESTIONS RELATING TO INDIVIDUALS

Marital status (Scottish Qn 2). Retains the traditional four categories
'Single', 'Married', 'Widowed', 'Divorced' with no distinction between
'1st Marriage' and 'Re-married'.

Language (Scottish Gaelic) asked in Scotland only. For all persons aged 3
or over (born before 6 April 1978):
Can the person speak, read or write Scottish Gaelic? Please tick the
appropriate box:
1☐Can speak Gaelic
2☐Can read Gaelic
3☐Can write Gaelic
4☐Does not know Gaelic

2. WALES

Questions as for England, with one addition

Language (Welsh) asked in Wales only
For all persons aged 3 or over (born before 6 April 1978), please tick
the appropriate box
(a) Speaks Welsh   1☐Yes; 2☐No
(b) If 'Yes', 1☐speaks English; 2☐reads Welsh; 3☐writes Welsh

3. NORTHERN IRELAND

QUESTIONS RELATING TO THE HOUSEHOLD'S ACCOMMODATION

Sharing. A question similar to that used in England in 1971 (A2) is
retained: Do you share with any other household in the building the use of
any room, landing, hall, passage or staircase?
     1☐Yes   2☐No

Amenities. This question seeks much more extensive information than that
collected in Great Britain.
Has your household the use of the following amenities on these premises?
Please tick the appropriate boxes

     A fixed bath or shower permanently connected to a water supply and
     a waste pipe
     A flush toilet (W.C.) with entrance inside the building
     A flush toilet (W.C.) with entrance outside the building
     In each of the above cases
     1☐Yes - for use only by this household
     2☐Yes - for use also by another household
     3☐No

     Water supply:
     1☐Public supply piped into house
     2☐Public supply at a standpipe
     3☐Other

     Domestic sewage disposal:
     1☐Public sewer
     2☐Septic tank/cesspit
     3☐Dry closet/chemical toilet

     Central heating:
     1☐Yes
     2☐No

Which fuel or power is used to provide the main source of heating for your
household. (Please tick one box only.)
     1☐Solid fuels (includes coal, anthracite, wood, turf)
     2☐Electricity
     3☐Oil (includes paraffin)
     4☐Mains gas
     5☐Bottled gas
     6☐Other means; please specify ....

APPENDIX 2 (cont.)

Does your household have any of the following forms of heating insulation?
(More than one may be ticked.)
1☐ Roof space insulation
2☐ Cavity wall insulation
3☐ None

QUESTIONS RELATING TO INDIVIDUALS

Journey to work. In the absence of 'underground, tube, metro, etc.', this
category is omitted. An additional question is asked:
'Please state the time the journey to work usually starts'

Religion. Unique to Northern Ireland is the voluntary question:
'Please state the Religion, Religious Denomination or Body to which the
person belongs. The general term 'Protestant' should not be used alone and
the denomination should be given as precisely as possible.'

APPENDIX 3: TYPES AND NUMBERS OF AREAS FOR WHICH 1981 CENSUS DATA HAVE BEEN PRODUCED

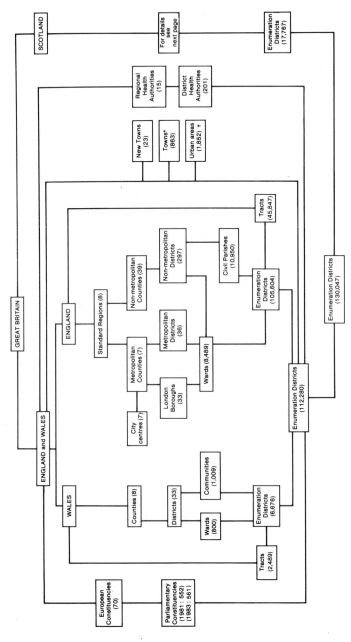

* Towns as constituted prior to the 1974 reorganisation of local government

\+ Urban areas specially defined for use with the 1981 census data

APPENDIX 3   (cont.) : SCOTLAND

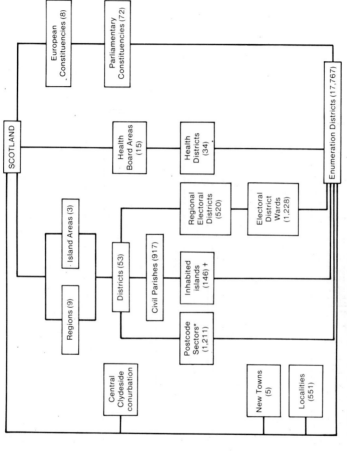

*   Where postcode sectors do not fit local government boundaries any
     sector falling into more than one L.A.A. is divided into parts and appears
     thus in the census reports

+   Many inhabited islands have populations below suppression level : full
     SAS are given only for 62 inhabited islands or agglomerations

49

APPENDIX 4 : STANDARD FORMAT OF THE 1981 SMALL AREA STATISTICS

CENSUS 1981 SMALL AREA STATISTICS

PAGE 1   100%

ED No:

Map Reference

Note: **#** = ED same as in 1971
       ## = Special Enumeration District

Crown copyright reserved [Frame No:

Separate explanatory notes are available

1 All persons present, plus absent residents = in private households

	TOTAL PERSONS	In private households		Not in private households	
		Males	Females	Males	Females
1 All present res	8	1	0	6	7
2 All res not res	13	17	18	xxx	xxx
3 All visitors	15	24	25	27	28
Res in UK	22	31	32	38	39
Res outside UK	36	38	39	41	42
ALL PRESENT 1981					
1971 BASE*[-33]	43	45	46	48	49
1981 RESID 1981					
1981 BASE*[+2]					

3 Persons present not in private households

Establishments	TOTAL PERS	Males (M)	Females (F)	Usually resident		Not usually resident Staff **		Other		Residents Staff **		Other	
				M	F	M	F	M	F	M	F	M	F
TOTAL #	210	211	212	214	215	217	218	219	220				
Hotels/boarding houses	221	222	223	225	226	228	229	230	231				
Children's homes	233	244	245	247	248	250	251	252	252				
Old people's homes	254	255	256	258	259	261	262	263	264				
Psychiatric hospitals	265	266	267	269	270	272	273	274	275				
Other hospitals													
Schools and colleges	276	277	278	280	281	283	284	285	286				
Prison dept. estabs	287	298	299	300	302	303	305	306	307				
Miscellaneous estabs	298	299	300	302	303	305	306	307	308				
Other establishments	309	310	311	313	314	316	317	318	319				

2 All residents

Age	TOTAL PERSONS	Males			Females			Ret'd Males
		SWD	Mr'd		SWD	Mr'd		
TOTAL	50	52	53		55	56		190
0-4	57	59	xxx		59	69		xxx
5-9	64	66	xxx		69	66		xxx
10-14	71	80	xxx		80	91		xxx
15-19	78	87	88		90	91		xxx
16-19	85	94	105		104	98		xxx
20-24	92							xxx
25-29	99	105	109		105	105		xxx
30-34	106	108	109		111	112		199
35-39	113	115	116		118	119		200
40-44	120	122	123		126	126		201
45-49	127	129	130		132	133		203
50-54	134	137	137		139	140		204
55-59	141	145	147		147	147		205
60-64	148	150	151		153	154		206
65-69	155	164	165		167	168		207
70-74	162	171	172		174	175		208
75-79	169							
80-84	183	185	186		188	182		
85+								

4 All residents

Country of birth	Males	Females
TOTAL	321	322
England	324	325
Scotland	327	328
Rest of UK	330	331
Irish Rep.	333	334
New Comm'th	336	337
New Comm'th	342	343
East Africa	345	346
Caribbean	351	352
India	354	355
Bangladesh	357	358
Far East	360	361
Mediterr	363	364
Remainder	366	367
Pakistan	369	370
Other E.C.	372	373
Other Europe	375	376
Rest of World	378	379

5 All residents aged 16 or over

Economic Position	TOTAL PERS	Males			Females		
		SWD	Mr'd		SWD	Mr'd	
ALL PERSONS 16+	380	382	383		380	385	386
Total econ active	387	396	397		397	399	400
Working	394	400	404		404	406	407
Seeking work	408	410	417		417	419	420
Total econ inact	415	424	425		425	427	428
Retired	429	431	432		432	434	435
Student	436	438	439		439	441	449
Other inactive	443	445			445	448	449

7 All residents aged 16 or over in employment

Employment status	Males		Females	
		SWD		SWD
ALL IN EMPLOYMENT	615	616	617	
Apprentices and trainees	618	619		
Employees supervising others	621	622	620	
Other employees	624	625	623	
Self-empl: no employees	627	628	626	
Self-empl: with employees	630	631	629	
ALL EMPLOYEES	633	634	635	
Working full-time	636	637	638	
Working part-time	639	640	641	

8 All residents aged 1 or over with a usual address 1 year before census different from present usual address

Age	TOTAL PERS	Males			Females			Not in employment
		SWD	Mr'd		SWD	Mr'd		
TOTAL	642	644	645		647			648
1-4	649	651	654		654			xxx
5-15	656	658	665		665			659
16-24	663	670	672		673	675		676
25-34	670	677	680		680	683		683
35-59	684	686	687		689	690		690
60-64	691	693	694		694	696		697
65+		700	701		703			704

NOTES

* Persons returned as usually resident but absent on census night in private household with one or more other persons present (Table 1)

\# Includes campers vagrants etc (Table 3)

** Includes relatives of staff (Table 3 and 6)

6 All persons present

Age	TOTAL PERSONS	In private households		Not in private households		All present		Staff **		Residents		Other	
	M	F	M	F	M	F	M	F	M	F	M	F	
TOTAL	450	452	453	455	456	457	458	459	460				
0-4	461	463	464	466	467	468	469	470	471				
5-15	472	474	475	477	478	479	480	481	482				
16-24	483	485	486	489	489	491	492	492	493				
25-34	496	497	499	500	501	502	503	504					
35-44	505	507	508	510	511	512	513	514	515				
45-54	516	518	519	521	522	523	524	525	526				
55-59	527	529	532	532	533	534	535	536	537				
60-64	538	540	541	543	545	546	547	548					
65-69	549	551	552	554	555	556	557	558	559				
70-74	560	562	563	565	566	567	578	579	580	581			
75+	571	573	574	576	577	578	579	580	581				
Single	582	584	585	587	588	589	590	591	592				
Married	593	595	596	598	599	600	601	602	603				
Students aged 16 or over	604	606	607	609	610	611	612	613	614				

9 All Economically Active (EA) residents

Age	TOTAL PERSONS EA	Males EA			Females EA			In emp working f/t		Not in employment		Self empl pers
		SWD	Mr'd		SWD	Mr'd		Males		Females		
								SWD	Mr'd	SWD	Mr'd	
TOTAL	720	722	723		723	728		790	792	793		705
16-19	724	727	732		732	728		795	797	798		706
20-24	729	732	737		737	738		800	802	803		707
25-29	736	739	742		742	743		805	810	812		708
30-34	739	742	743		743	745		810	812	813		709
35-39	740	745	747		747	747		815	818	818		710
40-44	745	752	752		752	758		820	822	822		711
45-49	755	757	758		758	758		825	828	828		712
50-54	754	760	762		762	763		830	832	833		713
55-59	760	762	763		763	763		833	900	902		714
60-64	769	770	772		772	773		840	842	843		715
65-69	775	777	778		778	778		845	847	848		716
70-74	780	782	783		783	788		850	852	855		717
75+	784	785	787		787	788		855	857	858		718

APPENDIX 4 (cont)

CENSUS 1981 SMALL AREA STATISTICS

PAGE 2   100%

ED No

Map Reference

Note: $ = ED same as in 1971
$$ = Special Enumeration District

Crown copyright reserved   Frame No:

Separate explanatory notes are available

10 Private households (H) with residents; residents (P)

Tenure		TOTALS	Bath and inside WC present — Both excl shared	One/both shared	Lack bath inside WC	Neither bath nor inside WC	Lack bath inside WC	Lack inside WC	Share inside WC	Persons per room >1.5	>1‑1.5	No car
ALL HOUSEHOLDS	H	929	930	931	932	933	934	935	936	945	946	949
	P	937	938	939	940	941	942	943	944	947	948	950
All permanent	H	951	952	953	954	955	956	957	958	967	968	971
	P	959	960	961	962	963	964	965	966	969	970	972
Owner occupied	H	973	974	975	976	977	978	979	980	989	990	993
	P	981	982	983	984	985	986	987	988	991	992	994
Council etc	H	995	996	997	998	999	1000	1001	1002	1011	1012	1015
	P	1003	1004	1005	1006	1007	1008	1009	1010	1013	1014	1016
Housing association	H	1017	1018	1019	1020	1021	1022	1023	1024	1033	1034	1037
	P	1025	1026	1027	1028	1029	1030	1031	1032	1035	1036	1038
Rented with business	H	1039	1040	1041	1042	1043	1044	1045	1046	1055	1056	1059
	P	1047	1048	1049	1050	1051	1052	1053	1054	1057	1058	1060
By virtue of employment	H	1061	1062	1063	1064	1065	1066	1067	1068	1077	1078	1081
	P	1069	1070	1071	1072	1073	1074	1075	1076	1079	1080	1082
Other rented unfurnished	H	1083	1084	1085	1086	1087	1088	1089	1090	1099	1100	1103
	P	1091	1092	1093	1094	1095	1096	1097	1098	1101	1102	1104
Other rented furnished	H	1105	1106	1107	1108	1109	1110	1111	1112	1121	1122	1125
	P	1113	1114	1115	1116	1117	1118	1119	1120	1123	1124	1126
Non-permanent	H	1127	1128	1129	1130	1131	1132	1133	1134	1143	1144	1147
	P	1135	1136	1137	1138	1139	1140	1141	1142	1145	1146	1148

11 Household spaces; rooms in household spaces

Occupancy Type	TOTAL H/HOLD SPACES	TOTAL ROOMS
ALL TYPES OF OCCUPANCY	1149	1159
H/hold enum with usual residents	1150	1160
Absent household	1151	1161
H/hold enum with no usual residents — Owner occupied	1152	1162
not owner occupied (unoccupied at Census)	1153	1163
Second/holiday accom 'unoccupied at Census'	1154	1164
Holiday accomm 'unoccupied at Census'	1155	1165
Vacant (new, never occupied)	1156	1166
Vacant (other, improvement)	1157	1167
Hotels and boarding houses	1158	1168
	xxx	1169

12 Private household with residents; residents; cars in households

	TOTALS	No car	1 car	2 cars	3 or more cars	TOTAL CARS*
Households	1170	1171	1172	1173	1174	1175
Persons in households	1176	1177	1178	1179	1180	xxx

* H/hlds with 3 or more cars are counted as having 3 cars

13 Private households (H) with residents; residents (P); rooms in household spaces

Tenure		TOTALS	Households with the following rooms: 1	2	3	4	5	6	7+	TOTAL ROOMS
All permanent	H	1182	1183	1184	1185	1186	1187	1188	1189	1190
	P	1191	1192	1193	1194	1195	1196	1197	1198	xxx
Owner occupied	H	1200	1201	1202	1203	1204	1205	1206	1207	1208
	P	1209	1210	1211	1212	1213	1214	1215	1216	xxx
Council etc	H	1218	1219	1220	1221	1222	1223	1224	1225	1226
	P	1227	1228	1229	1230	1231	1232	1233	1234	xxx
Housing association	H	1236	1237	1238	1239	1240	1241	1242	1243	1244
	P	1245	1246	1247	1248	1249	1250	1251	1252	xxx
Rented with business	H	1254	1255	1256	1257	1258	1259	1260	1261	1262
	P	1263	1264	1265	1266	1267	1268	1269	1270	xxx
By virtue of employment	H	1272	1273	1274	1275	1276	1277	1278	1279	1280
	P	1281	1282	1283	1284	1285	1286	1287	1288	xxx
Other rented unfurnished	H	1290	1291	1292	1293	1294	1295	1296	1297	1298
	P	1299	1300	1301	1302	1303	1304	1305	1306	xxx
Other rented furnished	H	1308	1309	1310	1311	1312	1313	1314	1315	1316
	P	1317	1318	1319	1320	1321	1322	1323	1324	xxx
Non-permanent	H	1326	1327	1328	1329	1330	1331	1332	1333	1334
	P	1335	1336	1337	1338	1339	1340	1341	1342	xxx

14 Private households with residents; residents; rooms in such h/holds

H/holds with the following persons	Households with the following rooms: 1	2	3	4	5	6	7+	TOTAL H/HOLDS	TOTAL ROOMS	TOTAL CARS*
ALL H/HOLDS	1344	1345	1346	1347	1348	1349	1350	1351	1352	1353
1	1354	1355	1356	1357	1358	1359	1360	1361	1362	1363
2	1364	1365	1366	1367	1368	1369	1370	1371	1372	1373
3	1374	1375	1376	1377	1378	1379	1380	1381	1382	1383
4	1384	1385	1386	1387	1388	1389	1390	1391	1392	1393
5	1394	1395	1396	1397	1398	1399	1400	1401	1402	1403
6	1404	1405	1406	1407	1408	1409	1410	1411	1412	1413
7+	1414	1415	1416	1417	1418	1419	1420	1421	1422	1423

	TOTAL PERS	Stat PERS AGED 16+	TOTAL ROOMS	TOTAL CARS*
TOTAL PERS	1416	1417	1418	1419 1420 1421 1422 1423

* H/hlds with 3 or more cars are counted as having 3 cars

15 Tenure of households in permanent buildings

H/holds with the following persons	All permanent	Owner occ	Council	H use assoc	Rented with business	By virtue of emp/assoc	Other rented Unfurn	Furn	Households not in perm accom
ALL H/HOLDS	1425	1426	1427	1428	1429	1430	1431	1432	1433
1	1434	1435	1436	1437	1438	1439	1440	1441	1442
2	1443	1444	1445	1446	1447	1448	1449	1450	1451
3	1452	1453	1454	1455	1456	1457	1458	1459	1460
4	1461	1462	1463	1464	1465	1466	1467	1468	1469
5	1470	1471	1472	1473	1474	1475	1476	1477	1478
6	1479	1480	1481	1482	1483	1484	1485	1486	1487
7+	1488	1489	1490	1491	1492	1493	1494	1495	1496

16 Priv h/holds with pers present but no residents; pers present rooms and cars in such h/holds

	TOTAL H/HOLDS	Bath + inside wc excl	Stat PERS AGED 16+	TOTAL PERS	TOTAL ROOMS	TOTAL CARS*
H/holds with pers present, no res persons	1497	1498	1499	1500	1501	1502

17

Line 1: 1971 pop base
Line 2: 1981 pop base; 1981 private household base*

	0	1	2	3	4	5	6	7+	TOTAL HOUSE-HOLDS	TOTAL ROOMS (1981)	TOTAL PERS (1981)
Line 1	1503	1504	1505	1506	1507	1508	1509	1510	1511	1512	1513
Line 2	1514	1515	1516	1517	1518	1519	1520	1521	1522	1523	1524

* Private households with 1 or more usual residents with at least 1 person (a resident or a visitor) present, or with a visitor or visitors present but no usual residents in a household with '0 persons'

PAGE 3   CENSUS 1981 SMALL AREA STATISTICS   100%

E No

Map Reference

Note: $ = ED name as in 1971
        $$ = Special Enumeration District

Crown copyright reserved Frame No:

Separate explanatory notes are available

NOTES

* Persons aged 16 or over (Tables 18 and 22)
** Includes household with no persons usually
   resident aged 18 or over (Table 18)
Includes residents in households with heads
   counted in the 16-28 row (Table 26)
Includes residents in households with heads
   aged under 16 (Table 26)

18 Private households with residents: residents

Households with the following adults *	House-holds with no person aged 0-15	Households with persons aged 0-15				Persons in households			
		House-holds	With one person aged 0-15		With two or more aged 0-15		With no person aged 0-15	With persons aged 0-15	
			Aged 0-4	Aged 5-15	All Aged 0-4	All Aged 5-15	Oth- ers	Pers econ act	Pers aged 0-15	Pers econ act	Pers aged 16+
								TOTAL PERS			
ALL HOUSEHOLDS **	1525	1526	1527	1528	1529	1530	1531	574	1575	1576	1577	1578
1 Male	1532	1533	1534	1535	1536	1537	1538	579	1580	1581	1582	1583
1 Female	1539	1540	1541	1542	1543	1544	1545	584	1585	1586	1587	1588
2 (Married male + married female)	1546	1547	1548	1549	1550	1551	1552	589	1590	1591	1592	1593
2 (Other)	1553	1554	1555	1556	1557	1558	1559	594	1595	1596	1597	1598
3+ (Married male(s)+ married female(s)) with or without others)	1560	1561	1562	1563	1564	1565	1566	599	1600	1601	1602	1603
3+ (Other)	1567	1568	1569	1570	1571	1572	1573	1604	1605	1606	1607	1608

20 Residents aged 18 or over in private households

Economic position	TOTAL PERS	Males			Females		
		Mrr'd	SWD	Mrr'd	Mrr'd	SWD	Mrr'd
ALL PERSONS 16+	1629	1630	1631	1632	1633		
Total econ act	1638	1639	1640	1641	1642	1643	
Working f/time	1644	1645	1646	1647	1648		
Working p/time	1649		1654	1655	1656		
Temp sick	1654		1660	1661	1662		
Total econ inact	1659	1660	1670	1671	1672		
Retired	1664	1665	1675	1676	1677		
Student	1669	1670	1680	1681	1682		
Other inactive	1674	1675					

21 Residents in private households

Age	TOTAL PERSONS	Males		Females		
		Mrr'd	SWD	Mrr'd	SWD	Mrr'd
TOTAL	1684	1686	1687	1689	1690	
0-4	1691					
5-9	1695	1703	xxx	xxx	1703	xxx
10-14	1705	1707	xxx	xxx	1710	xxx
15	1712	1714	xxx	xxx	1717	xxx
16-19	1719	1721	1722	1724	1725	
20-24	1726	1728	1729	1731	1738	
25-29	1733	1735	1736	1738	1739	
30-34	1740	1742	1743	1745	1746	
35-39	1747	1749	1750	1752	1753	
40-44	1754	1756	1757	1759	1760	
45-49	1761	1763	1764	1766	1767	
50-54	1768	1770	1771	1773	1774	
55-59	1775	1777	1778	1780	1781	
60-64	1782	1784	1785	1787	1788	
65-69	1789	1791	1792	1794	1795	
70-74	1796	1798	1799	1801	1802	
75-79	1803	1805	1806	1808	1809	
80-84	1810	1812	1813	1815	1816	
85+	1817	1819	1820	1822	1823	

19 Married women resident in private household of married male plus one married female with or without others: number of persons aged 0-16 in such households

In households with:	TOTAL MRR'D WOMEN	Mrr'd women econ ACTIVE	Mrr'd women in employment	
			Working full-time	Working pt-time
No person aged 0-15	1609	1610	1617	1618
Person(s) aged 0-4 with or without person(s) aged 5-15	1611	1612	1620	1621
Person(s) aged 5-15 only	1613	1614	1623	1624
TOTAL PERSONS AGED 0-15	1615	1616	1626	1627

23 Married women resident Married women in empl

Age	TOTAL MARRIED WOMEN	Married women econ active	TOTAL	Work hours f/time	Work hours p/time
TOTAL	1878	1879	1890	1891	1892
16-24	1880	1881	1893	1894	1895
25-34	1882	1883	1896	1897	1898
35-44	1884	1885	1900	1901	1904
45-59	1886	1887	1902	1903	1904
60+	1888	1889	1905	1906	1907

22 Private households with residents: residents aged 16 or over

Households with the following persons aged 16 or over *	Households with the following persons aged 0-15				
	0	1	2	3	4+
	TOTAL	Males	Males	Males	Males
TOTAL HOUSEHOLDS	1824	1826	1828	1829	
1 econ active/	1830	1831	1832	1834	1835
2+, all econ inac	1842	1843	1844	1846	1847
2+, 1 econ active	1848	1849	1850	1852	1853
2+, 2+ econ active	1854	1856	1858	1859	

24 Residents aged 16-24 in private households

Age	Persons		Married		Student		Econ active		EA out of empl	
	Males	Males	Males	Males	Males	Males	Males	Males	Males	Males
TOTAL	1908	1909	1928	1929	1948	1949	1968	1969	1988	1989
16	1910	1911	1930	1931	1950	1951	1970	1971	1990	1991
17	1912	1913	1932	1933	1952	1953	1972	1973	1992	1993
18	1914	1915	1934	1935	1954	1955	1974	1975	1994	1995
19	1916	1917	1936	1937	1956	1957	1976	1977	1996	1997
20	1918	1919	1938	1939	1958	1959	1978	1979	1998	1999
21	1920	1921	1940	1941	1960	1961	1980	1981	2000	2001
22	1922	1923	1942	1943	1962	1963	1982	1983	2002	2003
23	1924	1925	1944	1945	1964	1965	1984	1985	2004	2005
24	1926	1927	1946	1947	1966	1967	1986	1987	2006	2007

25 Residents aged 0-15 in private households

Age	Males	Females
TOTAL	2009	2010
0	2012	2013
1	2015	2016
2	2018	2019
3	2021	2022
4	2024	2025
5	2027	2028
6	2030	2031
7	2033	2034
8	2036	2037
9	2039	2040
10	2042	2043
11	2045	2046
12	2048	2049
13	2051	2052
14	2054	2055
15	2057	2058

26 Residents in private households

Age	TOTAL	Males			Females		
		Mrr'd	S	W/D	Mrr'd	S	W/D
PERSONS AGED 16 OR OVER IN PRIVATE HOUSEHOLDS	2059	2061	2062	2063	2065	2066	2067
ALL 16+	2068	2070	2071	2072	2074	2075	2076
16-29	2077	2079	2080	2081	2083	2084	2085
30-44	2086	2088	2089	2090	2092	2093	2094
45-64/59	2095	2097	2098	2099	2101	2102	2103
Pensioners							
HEADS IN PRIVATE HOUSEHOLDS	2104	2106	2107	2108	2110	2111	2112
ALL 16+	2113	2115	2116	2117	2119	2120	2121
16-29	2122	2124	2125	2126	2128	2129	2130
30-44	2131	2133	2134	2135	2137	2138	2139
45-64/59	2140	2142	2143	2144	2146	2147	2148
Pensioners							
ALL PERS IN PRIVATE HOUSEHOLDS BY M/S,SEX, MAR.STAT	2149	2151	2152	2153	2155	2156	2157
HEADS AGED: ALL 16+	2158	2160	2161	2162	2164	2165	2166
16-29	2167	2169	2170	2171	2173	2174	2175
30-44	2176	2178	2179	2180	2182	2183	2184
45-64/59	2185	2187	2188	2189	2191	2192	2193
Pensioners							

APPENDIX 4 (cont)

CENSUS 1981 SMALL AREA STATISTICS
PAGE 4   100%

ED No

Map Reference

Note: * = ED same as in 1971
$$ = Special Enumeration District

Crown copyright reserved   Frame No:

Separate explanatory notes are available

NOTES

*Persons aged 18 and over (Tables 27 + 31)

Inc households with no persons usually resident aged 18 and over (Table 29)

*inc renting from LAs, New Town Corporations and Scottish Special Housing Assoc (Table 29)

---

27 Lone adults - residents in private households of one adult with residents aged 0-15, number of persons aged 0-15 in such households

In households with child(ren):

	Male lone 'parents'					Female lone 'parents'				
	TOTAL	Econ active	In employment TOTAL	F/time	P/time	TOTAL	Econ active	In employment TOTAL	F/time	P/time
Aged 0-4 with or w/out any 5-15	2194	2195	2196	2197	2198	2199	2200	2201	2202	2203
Aged 5-15 only	2204	2205	2206	2207	2208	2209	2210	2211	2212	2213
TOTAL PERSONS AGED 0-15	2214	2215	2216	2217	2218	2219	2220	2221	2222	2223

---

28 Private households with residents not in self-contained accommodation: rooms in such households

Households with residents not in self-contained accommodation

Households with the following persons	TOTAL	One or more persons per rm	Bath+ inside WC excl	Lack inside WC	Lack bath excl	No car	TOTAL ROOMS
TOTAL	2224	2228	2232	2233	2234	2248	2244
1 person	2225	2229	2235	2236	2237	2249	2245
2 persons	2226	2230	2238	2239	2240	2250	2246
3+ persons	2227	2231	2241	2242	2243	2251	2247

---

29 Private h/holds with residents, residents aged 0-15, and aged 60+ (females) and 65+ (males)

Household type / Households with persons

Household type	Aged 0-15	TOTAL HOUSEHOLDS	Tenure of households in permanent buildings							House-holds in non-perm accom
			TOTAL	Owner occ	Rented Coun-cil etc	Hou-sing assoc	Rented with job/bus-iness of empl	Other rented Unfurn	Furn	
ALL HOUSEHOLDS	Any	2252	2262	2263	2264	2265	2266	2267	2268	2342
1 pensioner / 1 adult under pensionable age	0	2253	2270	2271	2272	2273	2274	2275	2276	2343
	0	2254	2278	2279	2280	2281	2282	2283	2284	2344
1 adult any age	1+	2255	2286	2287	2288	2289	2290	2291	2292	2345
marr'd male with / females without others	0	2256	2294	2295	2296	2297	2298	2299	2300	2346
	1+	2257	2302	2303	2304	2305	2306	2307	2308	2347
3+, marr'd males / females with / without others	0	2258	2310	2311	2312	2313	2314	2315	2316	2348
	1+	2259	2318	2319	2320	2321	2322	2323	2324	2349
2+ Others	0	2260	2326	2327	2328	2329	2330	2332	2333	2350
Households containing pers of pens age only (any number)	0	2261	2334	2335	2336	2337	2338	2339	2340	2351

(Additional cell references: 2269, 2277, 2285, 2293, 2301, 2309, 2317, 2325, 2333, 2341; non-perm accom 2342–2361)

---

30 Private h/holds with resident head with different address 1 year before census; all residents in such h/holds; all residents in private h/holds with different address 1 yr before census

	TOTAL	One or more persons per rm	Bath+ inside WC excl	Lack inside WC	Not self-cont accom	No car	
Households with migrant heads							
Households	2402	2404	2406	2407	2408	2412	2414
Persons	2403	2405	2409	2410	2411	2413	2415
Households with migrants							
All migrants	2416	2417	2418	2419	2420	2421	2422

---

31 Private households with dependent children; private households with one or more residents aged 0-15; residents in such households

Households with children

	TOTAL	One or more persons per rm	Bath+ inside WC excl	Lack inside WC	Lack bath	Not self-cont accom	No car
ALL H/HOLDS WITH DEPENDENT CHILD(REN)	2423	2424	2425	2426	2427	2428	2429
H/holds containing at least one lone parent family with dep child(ren)	2430	2431	2432	2433	2434	2435	2436
H/holds with 3 or more dep children	2437	2438	2439	2440	2441	2442	2443
ALL H/HOLDS WITH ONE OR MORE PERSONS AGED 0-15	2444	2453	2462	2471	2480	2489	2498
H/holds AGED 0-15	2445	2454	2463	2472	2481	2490	2499
Households / Persons 0-4	2446	2455	2464	2473	2482	2491	2500
Persons 5-15	2447	2456	2465	2474	2483	2492	2501
Other h/holds with persons 0-15	2448	2457	2466	2475	2484	2493	2502
Households	2449	2458	2467	2476	2485	2494	2503
Persons 0-4	2450	2459	2468	2477	2486	2495	2504
Persons 5-15	2451	2460	2469	2478	2487	2496	2505
H/holds with 3 or more persons 0-15	2452	2461	2470	2479	2488	2497	2506

---

32 Private households with one or more residents of pensionable age; residents in such households

Households with pensioners

	TOTAL	One or more persons per room	Bath+ inside WC excl	Lack inside WC	Not self-cont accom	No car	
TOTAL H/HOLDS WITH 1 OR MORE PENSIONERS	2507	2516	2525	2526	2527	2552	2561
Lone male 65-74	2508	2517	2528	2529	2530	2553	2562
Lone male 75+	2509	2518	2531	2532	2533	2554	2563
Lone female 60-74	2510	2519	2534	2535	2536	2555	2564
Lone female 75+	2511	2520	2537	2538	2539	2556	2565
2+ all pens <75	2512	2521	2540	2541	2542	2557	2566
2+, all pens, any 75+	2513	2522	2543	2544	2545	2558	2567
1 or more pens with 1 or more non-pensioner	2514	2523	2546	2547	2548	2559	2568
1 or more pens with 2 or more non-pens	2515	2524	2549	2550	2551	2560	2569
TOTAL PERS IN H/HOLDS WITH PENSIONERS	2570	2574	2578	2579	2580	2590	2594
Total pens persons 60-74	2571	2575	2581	2582	2583	2591	2595
Total pens persons 75+	2572	2576	2584	2585	2586	2592	2596
Total persons 85+	2573	2577	2587	2588	2589	2593	2597

APPENDIX 4 (cont)

CENSUS 1981 SMALL AREA STATISTICS

PAGE 5   10%

ED No

Map Reference

Note: $ = ED name as in 1971
      $$ = Special Enumeration District
      + = Importing Enumeration District

Crown copyright reserved   Frame No:

Separate explanatory notes are available

The figures in these tables are a 10% sample of the Census

44 Residents aged 16 or over in employment (10% sample)

Socio-economic group (SEG)	Agric	Energy and water	Constr	Manuf	Distrib and Catering	Trans-port	Other Services	TOTAL IN EMPL	Working full time	Working part time	Working working dist of residence
1	4223	4224	4225	4226	4227	4228	4229	4230	4375	4394	4413
2	4231	4232	4233	4234	4235	4236	4237	4238	4376	4395	4414
3	4239	4240	4241	4242	4243	4244	4245	4246	4377	4396	4415
4	4247	4248	4249	4250	4251	4252	4253	4254	4378	4397	4416
5-1	4255	4256	4257	4258	4259	4260	4261	4262	4379	4398	4417
5-2	4263	4264	4265	4266	4267	4268	4269	4270	4380	4399	4418
6	4271	4272	4273	4274	4275	4276	4277	4278	4381	4400	4419
7	4279	4280	4281	4282	4283	4284	4285	4286	4382	4401	4420
8	4287	4288	4289	4290	4291	4292	4293	4294	4383	4402	4421
9	4295	4296	4297	4298	4299	4300	4301	4302	4384	4403	4422
10	4303	4304	4305	4306	4307	4308	4309	4310	4385	4404	4423
11	4311	4312	4313	4314	4315	4316	4317	4318	4386	4405	4424
12	4319	4320	4321	4322	4323	4324	4325	4326	4387	4406	4425
13	4327	4328	4329	4330	4331	4332	4333	4334	4388	4407	4426
14	4335	4336	4337	4338	4339	4340	4341	4342	4389	4408	4427
15	4343	4344	4345	4346	4347	4348	4349	4350	4390	4409	4428
16	4351	4352	4353	4354	4355	4356	4357	4358	4391	4410	4429
17	4359	4360	4361	4362	4363	4364	4365	4366	4392	4411	4430
TOTAL	4367	4368	4369	4370	4371	4372	4373	4374	4393	4412	4431
Working outside distr of residence	4432	4433	4434	4435	4436	4437	4438	4439	4440	4441	xxx

45 Residents, private households with residents (100% + 10% sample)

	TOTAL IN EMPL	Not in private h/holds	Resident persons in private h/holds	PRIVATE H/HOLDS
100%	4442	4443	4444	4445
10%	4446	4447	4448	4449

46 Residents aged 16 or over in employment (10% sample)

Sex	TOTAL IN EMPL	Agric	Energy and water	Manuf	Constr	Distrib and Catering	Trans-port	Other Services
Males 16+	4450	4451	4452	4453	4454	4455	4456	4457
16-29	4458	4459	4460	4461	4462	4463	4464	4465
30-44	4466	4467	4468	4469	4470	4471	4472	4473
45-64	4474	4475	4476	4477	4478	4479	4480	4481
65+	4482	4483	4484	4485	4486	4487	4488	4489
Female 16+	4490	4491	4492	4493	4494	4495	4496	4497
16-29	4498	4499	4500	4501	4502	4503	4504	4505
30-44	4506	4507	4508	4509	4510	4511	4512	4513
45-59	4514	4515	4516	4517	4518	4519	4520	4521
60+	4522	4523	4524	4525	4526	4527	4528	4529

47 Residents aged 16 or over in employment (10% sample)

Means of travel to work

SEG	Car pool	Car (pass)	Car (driver)	Bus	BR train	Under-ground train	Motor-cycle	Pedal-cycle	On foot	Other foot/r/s	Works at home
1	4530	4531	4532	4533	4534	4535	4536	4537	4538	4539	4540
2	4541	4542	4543	4544	4545	4546	4547	4548	4549	4550	4551
3	4552	4553	4554	4555	4556	4557	4558	4559	4560	4561	4562
5-1	4563	4564	4565	4566	4567	4568	4569	4570	4571	4572	4573
5-2	4574	4575	4576	4577	4578	4579	4580	4581	4582	4583	4584
6	4585	4586	4587	4588	4589	4590	4591	4592	4593	4594	4595
7	4596	4597	4598	4599	4600	4601	4602	4603	4604	4605	4606
8	4607	4608	4609	4610	4611	4612	4613	4614	4615	4616	4617
9	4618	4619	4620	4621	4622	4623	4624	4625	4626	4627	4628
10	4629	4630	4631	4632	4633	4634	4635	4636	4637	4638	4639
11	4640	4641	4642	4643	4644	4645	4646	4647	4648	4649	4650
12	4651	4652	4653	4654	4655	4656	4657	4658	4659	4660	4661
13	4662	4663	4664	4665	4666	4667	4668	4669	4670	4671	4672
14	4673	4674	4675	4676	4677	4678	4679	4680	4681	4682	4683
15	4684	4685	4686	4687	4688	4689	4690	4691	4692	4693	4694
16	4695	4696	4697	4698	4699	4700	4701	4702	4703	4704	4705
Total pers	4706	4707	4708	4709	4710	4711	4712	4713	4714	4715	4716
Total male	4717	4718	4719	4720	4721	4722	4723	4724	4725	4726	4727
Total fmle	4728	4729	4730	4731	4732	4733	4734	4735	4736	4737	4738
	4739	4740	4741	4742	4743	4744	4745	4746	4747	4748	4749
	4750	4751	4752	4753	4754	4755	4756	4757	4758	4759	4760
Persons working or daily visitor or resid	4761	4762	4763	4764	4765	4766	4767	4768	4769	4770	xxx

Persons in employment in private households with:

	Car pool	Car (pass)	Car (driver)	Bus	BR train	Under-ground train	Motor-cycle	Pedal-cycle	On foot	Other foot/r/s	Works at home
No car or resid	4772	4773	4774	4775	4776	4777	4778	4779	4780	4781	4782
1 car	4783	4784	4785	4786	4787	4788	4789	4790	4791	4792	4793
2+ cars	4794	4795	4796	4797	4798	4799	4800	4801	4802	4803	4804

48 Residents aged 18 or over (10% sample)

Persons with degrees, professional and vocational qualifications

Age	TOTAL	Males	Females
18-29	4805	4806	4807
30-44	4808	4809	4810
45-59	4811	4812	4813
Pensioners	4814	4815	4816
In employment	4817	4818	4819

APPENDIX 4 (cont)

CENSUS 1981 SMALL AREA STATISTICS

PAGE 6   10%

ED No

Map Reference

Note: # = ED same as in 1971
      * = Special Enumeration District
      + = Importing Enumeration District

Crown copyright reserved   Frame No:

Separate explanatory notes are available

The figures in these tables are a 10% sample
of the Census

50 Residents, economically active or retired (10% sample)

SEG	All res econ active retired		Econ not in emp		Econ active			Econ active mig- rant
	Males	Females	Males	Females SWD	Males	Mrrd	SWD	
1	5147	5166	5167	5168	5223	5242	5243	5244	5299
2	5148	5169	5170	5171	5224	5245	5246	5247	5300
3	5149	5172	5175	5176	5225	5248	5251	5252	5301
4	5150	5175	5176	5177	5226	5251	5252	5253	5302
5-1	5151	5178	5179	5180	5227	5254	5255	5256	5303
5-2	5152	5181	5182	5183	5228	5257	5258	5259	5304
6	5153	5184	5185	5186	5229	5260	5261	5262	5305
7	5154	5187	5188	5189	5230	5263	5264	5265	5306
8	5155	5190	5191	5192	5231	5266	5267	5268	5307
9	5156	5193	5194	5195	5232	5269	5270	5271	5308
10	5157	5196	5197	5198	5233	5272	5273	5274	5309
11	5158	5199	5200	5201	5234	5275	5276	5277	5310
12	5159	5202	5203	5204	5235	5278	5279	5280	5311
13	5160	5205	5206	5207	5236	5281	5282	5283	5312
14	5161	5208	5209	5210	5237	5284	5285	5286	5313
15	5162	5211	5212	5213	5238	5287	5288	5289	5314
16	5163	5214	5215	5216	5239	5290	5291	5292	5315
TOTAL	5164	5217	5218	5219	5240	5293	5294	5295	5316

51 Residents aged 16 or over in employment (10% sample)

Employment Status	TOTAL IN EMPL	Selected industries				
		Agric. (forest +fishing)	Forestry fishing	Manuf	Constr	
Males						
Self-emp with empl	5318	5328	5329	5330	5331	
Self-emp w/o empl	5319	5342	5343	5344	5345	
Employees	5320	5349	5350	5351	5352	
Females						
Self-emp with empl	5322	5356	5357	5358	5359	
Self-emp w/o empl	5323	5363	5364	5365	5366	
Employees	5325	5370	5377	5378	5379	5380
Working full-time	5326	5377	5384	5385	5386	5387
Working part-time		5384	5391	5392	5393	5394

Selected industries continued:

	Distrib catering	Fin- ance	Pub admin other services		
	5332	5333	5334		
	5346	5347	5348		
	5353	5354	5355		
	5360	5361	5362		
	5367	5368	5369		
	5381	5382	5383		
	5388	5389	5390		
	5395	5396			

NOTES

Retired 1 = retired [head], previous occupation stated (Tables 49 and 52)
Retired 2 = retired [head] (no previous occupation stated) * never active [head] - in household
Retired 3 = retired [head] (no previous occupation stated) * never active person [self] - in household/[self] without an economically active person (Tables 49 and 52)

49 * households with residents; residents; families; families of resident persons (10% sample)

	Households					
	Selected tenures of h/hlds in perm bldgs			Migrant h/hold	No car	Ret head of h/hold
	Owner occ	Council occ	Unfurn- ished			
SEG						
				By SEG of EA or retired (with previous occupation stated) head of household		
1	4820	4821	4822	4877	4896	4915
2	4823	4824	4825	4879	4897	4916
3	4826	4827	4828	4880	4898	4917
4	4829	4830	4831	4881	4899	4918
5-1	4832	4833	4834	4882	4900	4919
5-2	4835	4836	4837	4883	4901	4920
6	4838	4839	4840	4884	4902	4921
7	4841	4842	4843	4885	4903	4922
8	4844	4845	4846	4885	4904	4923
9	4847	4848	4849	4886	4905	4924
10	4850	4851	4852	4887	4906	4925
11	4853	4854	4855	4888	4907	4926
12	4856	4857	4858	4889	4908	4927
13	4859	4860	4861	4890	4909	4928
14	4862	4863	4864	4891	4910	4929
15	4865	4866	4867	4892	4911	4930
16	4870	4872	4873	4894	4913	4932
17	4874	4875	4876	4895	4914	4933
Total (inc never act)						

52 Residents in private households, private households (10% sample)

	H/hlds and Residents in h/hlds				
Social class	House- holds	Per- sons	Mrrd Pers fmls	Pers 0-15	Pers 65+
I	5399	5412	5413	5414	
II	5398	5411	5415	5416	5417
IIIN	5400	5415	5417	5418	
IIIM	5401	5418	5423	5424	
IV	5402	5421	5422	5423	
V	5403	5424	5425	5426	
Armed forces	5404	5427	5428	5429	

53 Residents economically active but not in employment (10% sample)

	Former industry					
	Agric	Energy and water	Manuf	Constr	Distrib and catering	Trans- port
Males	5497	5498	5499	5500	5501	5502
NWF females	5504	5505	5506	5507	5508	
Mrrd females	5511	5512	5513	5514	5515	5516

OPCS GRO(S) Crown Copyright Reserved

55

APPENDIX 4 (cont)

CENSUS 1981 SMALL AREA STATISTICS

PAGE 7   100%

ED No

Map Reference

Note: $ = ED same as in 1971. $$ = Special Enumeration District

Crown copyright reserved   Frame No:

Separate explanatory notes are available

33 Household spaces; permanent buildings; non-permanent accommodation

| | Household spaces in permanent buildings with: | | | | | | | | | | Non-perm accom | |
| | Self-contained accommodation | | | | | | Not self-contained accom with shared entrance from o/side the building | | | | |
TOTAL H/HOLD SPACES	TOTAL	Purpose built flats	Sep entrance from o/side bldg	Shared entrance from outside the building: 2-rooms bath+inside WC excl	Flat-lets	Other	Total	Bed sits	Other	Cara vans	Other non-perm
TOTAL HOUSEHOLD SPACES 2598	2599	2600	2601	xxx	xxx	xxx	2605	xxx	xxx	2608	2609
Resident household spaces 2610	2611	2612	2613	2614	2615	2616	2617	2618	2619	2620	2621
Other household spaces 2622	2623	2624	2625	xxx	xxx	xxx	2629	xxx	xxx	2632	2633

34 Resident household spaces: rooms; residents in private households

| | | Household spaces in permanent buildings | | | | | Non-perm accom* |
	TOTAL	Purp-built flats	Sep entr-ance from o/side bldg	Self-cont accom	Shrd entrance from o/s bldg	Not self-cont accom	
TOTAL ROOMS	2634	2635	2636	2637	2638		2674
Rooms:							
1	2639	2640	2641	2642	2643		2675
2	2644	2645	2646	2647	2648		2676
3	2649	2650	2651	2652	2653		2677
4	2654	2655	2656	2657	2658		2678
5/6	2659	2660	2661	2662	2663		2679
7/8	2664	2665	2666	2667	2668		xxx
9+	2669	2670	2671	2672	2673		xxx
TOTAL PERSONS	2682	2683	2684	2685	2686		2722
Persons usually resident:							
1	2687	2688	2689	2690	2691		2723
2	2692	2693	2694	2695	2696		2724
3	2697	2698	2699	2700	2701		2725
4	2702	2703	2704	2705	2706		2726
5	2707	2708	2709	2710	2711		2727
6	2712	2713	2714	2715	2716		2728
7+	2717	2718	2719	2720	2721		2729
Persons per room:							
Greater than 1.5	2730	2731	2732	2733	2734		2755
>1 - 1.5	2735	2736	2737	2738	2739		2756
>0.5	2740	2741	2742	2743	2744		2757
0.5 or under	2745	2746	2747	2748	2749		2758
TOTAL H/HOLD SPACES	2750	2751	2752	2753	2754		2759

* Maximum number of persons in non-perm accom is five

35 Resident household spaces

| | | Household spaces in permanent buildings | | | | Non-perm accom |
| | | | | Shared entrance from o/s bldg | | |
	TOTAL	Purpose built flats	Separate entrance from outside building	Self-contained accom	Not self-contained accom	
Amenities: bath with:						
Exclusive inside WC	2760	2761	2762	2763	2764	2805
shared inside WC	2765	2766	2767	2768	2769	2806
no inside WC	2770	2771	2772	2773	2774	2807
Shared bath with:						
exclusive inside WC	2775	2776	2777	2778	2779	2808
shared inside WC	2780	2781	2782	2783	2784	2809
no inside WC	2785	2786	2787	2788	2789	2810
No bath with:						
exclusive inside WC	2790	2791	2792	2793	2794	2811
shared inside WC	2795	2796	2797	2798	2799	2812
no inside WC	2800	2801	2802	2803	2804	2813
Tenure:						
ALL TENURES	2814	2815	2816	2817	2818	2859
Owner occupied freehold	2819	2820	2821	2822	2823	2860
Owner occupied leasehold	2824	2825	2826	2827	2828	2861
Council, New Town, etc	2829	2830	2831	2832	2833	2862
Housing association	2834	2835	2836	2837	2838	2863
Rented with business	2839	2840	2841	2842	2843	2864
By virtue of employment	2844	2845	2846	2847	2848	2865
Other rented unfurnished	2849	2850	2851	2852	2853	2866
Other rented furnished	2854	2855	2856	2857	2858	2867

APPENDIX 4 (cont)

CENSUS 1981 SMALL AREA STATISTICS

ED No

Map Reference

Note: $ = ED same as in 1971.
$$ = Special Enumeration District

Crown copyright reserved | Frame No:

Separate explanatory notes are available

---

36 Private households with resident heads born in the New Commonwealth or Pakistan

| | New Commonwealth or Pakistan headed households | | | | | |
	TOTAL	1 or more persons per room	Bath + WC excl inside WC	Lack bath	Lack inside WC	Not in self cont accom	No car
Households	2868	2869	2870	2871	2872	2873	2874

---

37 Residents in private households

Birthplace of household head	TOTAL PERSONS	All ages In UK	All ages Outside UK	0-4 In UK	0-4 Outside UK	5-15 In UK	5-15 Outside UK	16-29 In UK	16-29 Outside UK	30-44 In UK	30-44 Outside UK	45 to pensionable age In UK	45 to pensionable age Outside UK	Pensionable age and over In UK	Pensionable age and over Outside UK	TOTAL HEADS OF HOUSEHOLDS
UK	2875	2876	2877	2878	2879	2880	2881	2882	2883	2884	2885	2886	2887	2888	2889	2950
Irish Republic	2890	2891	2892	2893	2894	2895	2896	2897	2898	2899	2900	2901	2902	2903	2904	2951
New Commonwealth and Pakistan	2905	2906	2907	2908	2909	2910	2911	2912	2913	2914	2915	2916	2917	2918	2919	2952
Rest of World	2920	2921	2922	2923	2924	2925	2926	2927	2928	2929	2930	2931	2932	2933	2934	2953
TOTAL	2935	2936	2937	2938	2939	2940	2941	2942	2943	2944	2945	2946	2947	2948	2949	2954

---

38 Households (H) with residents, rooms and resident persons (P) in owner occupied accommodation in permanent buildings

| Tenure | TOTAL HOUSEHOLDS | Households with the following rooms | | | | | | |
		1	2	3	4	5	6	7+
Freehold	2955	2956	2957	2958	2959	2960	2961	2962
Leasehold	2963	2964	2965	2966	2967	2968	2969	2970

| Tenure | Households with the following rooms | | | | | | | TOTALS | TOTAL ROOMS |
	1	2	3	4	5	6	7+		
F/hold H	2971	2972	2973	2974	2975	2976	2977	2978	2979
F/hold P	2980	2981	2982	2983	2984	2985	2986	2987	XXX
L/hold H	2988	2989	2990	2991	2992	2993	2994	2995	2996
L/hold P	2997	2998	2999	3000	3001	3002	3003	3004	3005

Tenure	TOTALS	Bath and inside WC present Both excl	Bath and inside WC present One/both shared	Lack inside WC nor bath	Neither inside WC or bath
TOTALS	3006	3007	3008	3009	3010
F/hold H	3011	3012	3013	3014	3015
F/hold P	3016	3017	3018	3019	3020
L/hold H	3021	3022	3023	3024	3025
L/hold P	3026	3027	3028	3029	3030

Tenure	Persons per room >1	Persons per room >1.5	Persons per room >1-1.5	No car
TOTALS	3031	3032	3033	3034
F/hold H	3035	3036	3037	3038
F/hold P	3039	3040	3041	3042
L/hold H	3043	3044	3045	3046
L/hold P	3047	3048	3049	3050

---

39 Persons aged 3 or over: Pres & abs h'hold residents

| Age | TOTAL PERSONS | Speaking Welsh | | | | Not Speaking Welsh |
		Not Speaking English Total	Not Speaking English Reads and writes Welsh	Speaking English Reads and writes Welsh	Speaking English Others	
3-4	3051	3052	3053	3054	3055	3056
5-15	3057	3058	3059	3060	3061	3062
16-24	3063	3064	3065	3066	3067	3068
25-44	3069	3070	3071	3072	3073	3074
45-64	3075	3076	3077	3078	3079	3080
65+	3081	3082	3083	3084	3085	3086
TOTAL RESIDENTS	3087	3088	3089	3090	3091	3092
Present residents and visitors (1981) (1971 Base)	3093	3094	3095	3096	3097	3098

APPENDIX 4 (cont)

40

CENSUS 1981 SMALL AREA STATISTICS
PAGE 9 ADDITIONAL TABLES FOR SCOTLAND

ED No

Map Reference

Note: $$ = Special Enumeration District

Crown copyright reserved | Frame No:

Separate explanatory notes are available

Age	Resident population		Gaelic speakers							
			Speaks,reads or writes Gaelic		Read		Read and write		Others	
	Male	Female	Male	Female	Male	Female	Male	Female	Male	Female
0 - 2	3099	3100	xxx	xxx	xxx	xxx	xxx	xxx	xxx	xxx
3 - 4	3109	3110	3111	3112	3113	3114	3115	3116	3117	3118
5 - 9	3119	3120	3121	3122	3123	3124	3125	3126	3127	3128
10 - 14	3129	3130	3131	3132	3133	3134	3135	3136	3137	3138
15 - 19	3139	3140	3141	3142	3143	3144	3145	3146	3147	3148
20 - 24	3149	3150	3151	3152	3153	3154	3155	3156	3157	3158
25 - 29	3159	3160	3161	3162	3163	3164	3165	3166	3167	3168
30 - 34	3169	3170	3171	3172	3173	3174	3175	3176	3177	3178
35 - 39	3179	3180	3181	3182	3183	3184	3185	3186	3187	3188
40 - 44	3189	3190	3191	3192	3193	3194	3195	3196	3197	3198
45 - 49	3199	3200	3201	3202	3203	3204	3205	3206	3207	3208
50 - 54	3209	3210	3211	3212	3213	3214	3215	3216	3217	3218
55 - 59	3219	3220	3221	3222	3223	3224	3225	3226	3227	3228
60 - 64	3229	3230	3231	3232	3233	3234	3235	3236	3237	3238
65 - 69	3239	3240	3241	3242	3243	3244	3245	3246	3247	3248
70 - 74	3249	3250	3251	3252	3253	3254	3255	3256	3257	3258
75+	3259	3260	3261	3262	3263	3264	3265	3266	3267	3268
ALL AGES	3269	3270	3271	3272	3273	3274	3275	3276	3277	3278
Aged 16+	3279	3280	3281	3282	3283	3284	3285	3286	3287	3288
Not in pvt.h/hlds	3289	3290	3291	3292	3293	3294	3295	3296	3297	3298
Born in Scotland	3299	3300	3301	3302	3303	3304	3305	3306	3307	3308

41

Households in permanent buildings - level and access

Household type and age of residents	Basement		Ground		1 or 2		3 or 4		5 or 6		7 - 9		10 and over
	All	Any ext stair	All	Any ext stair	All	Ext str only	All	With lift	All	With lift	All	With lift	All
1 pensionable aged under 75 male	3309	3310	3311	3312	3313	3314	3315	3316	3317	3318	3319	3320	3321
female	3322	3323	3324	3325	3326	3327	3328	3329	3330	3331	3332	3333	3334
1 pensionable aged 75 and over male	3335	3336	3337	3338	3339	3340	3341	3342	3343	3344	3345	3346	3347
female	3348	3349	3350	3351	3352	3353	3354	3355	3356	3357	3358	3359	3360
2 pensionable both aged under 75	3361	3362	3363	3364	3365	3366	3367	3368	3369	3370	3371	3372	3373
2 pensionable either aged 75 and over	3374	3375	3376	3377	3378	3379	3380	3381	3382	3383	3384	3385	3386
3 or more pensionable any aged under 75	3387	3388	3389	3390	3391	3392	3393	3394	3395	3396	3397	3398	3399
3 or more pensionable any aged 75 and over	3400	3401	3402	3403	3404	3405	3406	3407	3408	3409	3410	3411	3412
1 pensionable and 1 non-pensionable	3413	3414	3415	3416	3417	3418	3419	3420	3421	3422	3423	3424	3425
1 pensionable and 2 or more non-pensionable	3426	3427	3428	3429	3430	3431	3432	3433	3434	3435	3436	3437	3438
2 or more pensionable and 1 non-pensionable	3439	3440	3441	3442	3443	3444	3445	3446	3447	3448	3449	3450	3451
2 or more pensionable and 2 or more non-pensionable	3452	3453	3454	3455	3456	3457	3458	3459	3460	3461	3462	3463	3464
Children in household:													
1 adult with:													
1 or more children all aged 0-4	3465	3466	3467	3468	3469	3470	3471	3472	3473	3474	3475	3476	3477
2 or more children all aged 5-15	3478	3479	3480	3481	3482	3483	3484	3485	3486	3487	3488	3489	3490
2 or more children aged 0-4 and 5-15	3491	3492	3493	3494	3495	3496	3497	3498	3499	3500	3501	3502	3503
2 or more adults with:													
1 or more children all aged 0-4	3504	3505	3506	3507	3508	3509	3510	3511	3512	3513	3514	3515	3516
2 or more children all aged 5-15	3517	3518	3519	3520	3521	3522	3523	3524	3525	3526	3527	3528	3529
2 or more children aged 0-4 and 5-15	3530	3531	3532	3533	3534	3535	3536	3537	3538	3539	3540	3541	3542
TOTAL HOUSEHOLDS	3543	3544	3545	3546	3547	3548	3549	3550	3551	3552	3553	3554	3555
TOTAL PERSONS	3556	3557	3558	3559	3560	3561	3562	3563	3564	3565	3566	3567	3568
0 - 2	3569	3570	3571	3572	3573	3574	3575	3576	3577	3578	3579	3580	3581
0 - 4	3582	3583	3584	3585	3586	3587	3588	3589	3590	3591	3592	3593	3594
65-74 male	3595	3596	3597	3598	3599	3600	3601	3602	3603	3604	3605	3606	3607
60-74 female	3608	3609	3610	3611	3612	3613	3614	3615	3616	3617	3618	3619	3620
75+ male	3621	3622	3623	3624	3625	3626	3627	3628	3629	3630	3631	3632	3633
75+ female	3634	3635	3636	3637	3638	3639	3640	3641	3642	3643	3644	3645	3646
Permanently sick	3647	3648	3649	3650	3651	3652	3653	3654	3655	3656	3657	3658	3659

APPENDIX 4 (cont)

CENSUS 1981 SMALL AREA STATISTICS
PAGE 10 ADDITIONAL TABLES FOR SCOTLAND

ED No

Map Reference

Note: $1 = Special Enumeration District

Crown copyright reserved | Frame No:

Separate explanatory notes are available

42 Households in permanent buildings

Rooms	TOTAL	With ancillary kitchen							TOTAL	Without ancillary kitchen							Rooms
		Bath and WC Both excl	Both other	Exclu-sive WC	Bath +/or WC lacking	Occupancy norm +	0	-		Bath and WC Both excl	Both other	Exclu-sive WC	Bath +/or WC lacking	Occupancy norm +	0	-	
1	3660	3661	3662	3663	3664	3665	3666	3667	3724	3725	3726	3727	3728	3729	3730	3731	1
2	3668	3669	3670	3671	3672	3673	3674	3675	3732	3733	3734	3735	3736	3737	3738	3739	2
3	3676	3677	3678	3679	3680	3681	3682	3683	3740	3741	3742	3743	3744	3745	3746	3747	3
4	3684	3685	3686	3687	3688	3689	3690	3691	3748	3749	3750	3751	3752	3753	3754	3755	4
5	3692	3693	3694	3695	3696	3697	3698	3699	3756	3757	3758	3759	3760	3761	3762	3763	5
6	3700	3701	3702	3703	3704	3705	3706	3707	3764	3765	3766	3767	3768	3769	3770	3771	6
7+	3708	3709	3710	3711	3712	3713	3714	3715	3772	3773	3774	3775	3776	3777	3778	3779	7+
TOTAL	3716	3717	3718	3719	3720	3721	3722	3723	3780	3781	3782	3783	3784	3785	3786	3787	TOTAL

43

Households with persons-	Aged 0-15	TOTAL	House that is				Flat or rooms in permanent buildings				Bath and WC Both excl	Both other	Exclu-sive WC	Bath +/or WC lacking	Occupancy norm +	0	-1	-2 or more
Aged 16 and over			Total	Deta-ched	Semi-det	Terr-aced	Two storey	Low rise	High rise	Single with shop								
* ALL HOUSEHOLDS	Any	3788	3806	3807	3808	3809	3810	3811	3812	3813	3814	3815	3816	3817				
1 pensionable	0	3789																
1 adult non-pensionable	0	3790																
2 or more, none aged	0	3791																
Married M + married F only	1+	3792																
Married M + married F only	0	3793																
Married M + married F(s) with or without others	1+	3794																
Marr M(s) + Marr F(s) with or without others	0	3795																
Other 2 or more adults	1+	3796																
Other 2 or more adults	0	3797																
All prns only households	1+	3798																
All prns only households	0	3799																
TENURE																		
ALL TENURES		3800																
Owner occupier		3801																
Council, SSHA and New Town		3802																
Housing association		3803																
Rent with farm, shop etc		3804																
By virtue of employment		3805																
Other unfurnished																		
Other furnished																		
AMENITIES																		
Bath and WC exclusive use																		
Bath and WC other																		
Lacking one or both																		
Exclusive use																		
TOTAL ROOMS																		
TOTAL PERSONS IN HOUSEHOLDS																		
Persons aged 0-4																		
5-15																		
Pensionable aged -75+																		

Rooms breakdown (right-hand block):

Rooms	In non perm	with migrant head
1	4201	4212
2	4202	4213
3	4203	4214
4	4204	4215
5	4205	4216
6	4206	4217
7+	4207	4218
TOTAL		

* Includes households with no persons usually resident aged 16 and over

GRO(S) Crown Copyright Reserved

APPENDIX 5: PUBLISHED VOLUMES OF THE 1981 CENSUS, GREAT BRITAIN

(a) TEXT PAGE(S)	(b) TOPIC AND TITLE	(c) NOTES	(d) AGGREGATION LEVEL(S)	(e) No. of VOLS	(f) No. of PAGES	(g) % of OUTPUT
	A. PRELIMINARY REPORTS					
EW	Preliminary Report		4	1	26	
EW	Preliminary Report for Towns, urban and rural areas	Towns as defined by 1971 boundaries	7	1	39	
SC	Preliminary Report		1,4,6	1	64	
EW	Historical Tables		1,2,3	1	17	
SC	Historical Tables		1,3	1	9	
			Totals	5	155	0.8
	B. COUNTY (and similar) REPORTS					
EW	County Reports	2 vols (Pt 1:100%; Pt 2: 10%) per County (for standard tables, see Appendix 6)	4	108	6,986	
SC	Regional Reports	4 vols (Vols 1,2 as EW Pts 1,2; Vols 3,4 additional variables/areas) per Region + one vol for Islands Areas	4,6,7	40	1,692	
EW	New Towns Report	2 vols; tables as County Reports 1,2	7	2	297	
SC	New Towns Report	2 vols: tables as Regional Reports 1,2	7	2	75	
			Totals	152	9,050	48.8
	C. NATIONAL REPORTS					
	(i) Summary volumes					
GB	National Report	2 vols (Pts 1,2) ⎫ Tables as in County/Regional Reports 1,2	2	2	374	
SC	Scottish Summary	2 vols (Vols 1,2) ⎬	3	2	137	
WA	Report for Wales	Also published in Welsh ⎭		1	151	
GB	Key Statistics for Local Authorities	Tables arranged by Standard Regions	1,2,3,4	1	126	
GB	Key Statistics for Urban Areas	County/Region aggregates	2,3	1	139	
EW	Key Statistics for Urban Areas	Vols for: North, Midlands, SE, SW and Wales (Urban areas as defined for 1981)	7	4	355	
SC	Key Statistics for Localities	Localities as defined for 1981	7	1	75	
			Totals	12	1,357	7.3
	(ii) Topic volumes					
	Birthplace and Usual Residence					
GB	Country of Birth		1,2	1	164	
SC	County of Birth			1	85	
GB	Usual Residence		4	1	149	
			Totals	3	398	2.1
	Migration					
GB	National Migration	2 vols (Pt 1: 100%; Pt 2: 10%)	1,2,3	1	390	
SC	Migration Report	4 vols (1 & 2: 100%; 3 & 4: 10%)	3,4	4	627	
EW	Regional Migration	2 vols (Pt 1: 100%; Pt 2: 10%) per Standard Region	2,3,4	18	2,658	
			Totals	23	3,675	19.8

(a) TEXT PAGE(S)	(b) TOPIC AND TITLE	(c) NOTES	(d) AGGREGATION LEVEL(S)	(e) No. of VOLS	(f) No. of PAGES	(g) % of OUTPUT
	Housing, Households and Families					
	EW Housing and Households		1,2	1	592	
	SC Housing and Households Report		1,4	1	116	
	EW Household and Family Composition		1,2	1	190	
	SC Household and Family Composition			1	146	
	GB Communal Establishments		1,2	1	107	
			Totals	5	1,151	6.2
	Economic Activity					
	GB Economic Activity		1,2	1	557	
	SC Economic Activity		1	1	238	
			Totals	2	795	4.3
	Workplace & Transport to Work					
	EW Workplace & Transport to Work		4	1	555	
	SC Workplace & Transport to Work		4	1	356	
			Totals	2	911	4.9
	Language					
	SC Gaelic Report		4,5,6,7	1	88	
	WA Welsh Language in Wales	Also published in Welsh	4,5	1	50	
			Totals	2	138	0.7
	Others					
	GB Sex, Age and Marital Status		1,3	1	43	
	GB Persons of Pensionable Age		1,2,3	1	411	
	GB Qualified Manpower		1,2	1	443	
			Totals	3	897	4.8
		Topic Volumes Totals		40	7,965	43.0
		TOTAL CENSUS OUTPUT		209	18,527	100.0

EW: England & Wales
GB: Great Britain
SC: Scotland
WA: Wales

NOTES

Column (a): indicates the pages of this CATMOG where a description of the volume contents may be found

Column (b): this arrangement by topics has no official status

Column (d): the aggregation levels indicated here are: 1. Country level only; 2. Standard Regions and subdivisions thereof; 3. Counties; 4. Local Authority Areas (Districts); 5. Wards or Parishes; 6. Postcode Sectors (Scotland only); 7. Special areas (see also p. above). The code number indicates the smallest areas for which data are presented; where more than one number appears, different aggregation levels are used in different tables.

Column (f): pages of tables, excluding explanatory text, maps, etc.

APPENDIX 6: CENSUS 1981, ENGLAND AND WALES: STANDARD TABLES OF THE COUNTY REPORTS

TABLE   BASE 'POPULATION'   CHARACTERISTICS AND CROSS-TABULATIONS

PART 1 (100% TABLES)

General Tables

1.   Population present, 1891-1981   Numbers, inter-censal change
2.   Boundary changes 1.iv.1974 - 5.iv.1981   Area, population present
3.   Area, population present, 1961-1981   Numbers, inter-censal change

Demographic Characteristics

4.   Pop. in private households and not in private households   Present residents, absent residents, visitors x sex
5.   Pop. present in private households   Age, marital status, students 16+ x sex
     Pop. present not in private households   Age, marital status, students 16+ x status in establishment x sex
6.   Pop. usually resident   Age x marital status x sex
7.   Pop. usually resident in private households   Age x marital status x sex
8.   Children usually resident in private households   Age (single years) x sex
9.   Pop. not in private households   Type of establishment x status in establishment x sex
10. Pop. usually resident   Country of birth x sex
11. Pop. usually resident in private households   Born in or out of U.K. x age x birthplace of head of household

Economic Characteristics

12. Pop. usually resident aged 16+   Economic position x age x marital status x sex
13. Pop. usually resident aged 16+ in employment   Employment status x sex x marital status (women)
14. Pop. usually resident aged 16+ in private households   Economic position x marital status x sex
15. Pop. usually resident aged 16-24 in private households   Economic position, marital status x age (single years) x sex
16. Married females usually resident in private households   Economic position x age

Housing and Amenities

17. Household spaces   Occupancy type x household space type
18. Household spaces   Occupancy type x number of household spaces x total rooms
     Hotels and boarding houses   Total rooms
19. Private households with usual residents   No. of rooms in household, size of household, persons per room x household
                                                                           space type
20. Private households with usual residents   Tenure x household space type
21. Private households with usual residents   Amenities x household space type
22. Private households with population present   Population present, total rooms

62

APPENDIX 6 (cont.)

TABLE	BASE 'POPULATION'	CHARACTERISTICS AND CROSS-TABULATIONS
23.	Private households with population present	Population usually resident, total rooms
24.	Private households with usual residents	Tenure of households in permanent buildings, households in non-permanent accommodation x number of rooms in household
25.	Persons usually resident in private households	Tenure of households in permanent buildings, households in non-permanent accommodation x number of rooms in household
26.	Private households with usual residents	Size of household x tenure of households in permanent accommodation, households in non-permanent accommodation
27.	Private households with usual residents	Tenure of households in permanent buildings, households in non-permanent accommodation x amenities, persons per room, households with no car
28.	Persons usually resident in private households	Tenure of households in permanent buildings, households in non-permanent accommodation x amenities, persons per room, households with no car
29.	Private households with usual residents	Size of household x number of rooms in household
	Persons usually resident in private households	Number of rooms in household
30.	Private households with usual residents in not self-contained accommodation in permanent buildings	Size of household x amenities, density 1+ per room, total rooms, households with no car
31.	Private households with usual residents	Number of cars
	Persons usually resident in private households	Number of cars
32.	Private households with persons present but no usual residents	Amenities, persons present, students aged 16+, total rooms, total cars
33.	Private households with heads born in New Commonwealth or Pakistan	Amenities, in not self-contained accommodation, with no car, density 1+ per room

Household Composition

TABLE	BASE 'POPULATION'	CHARACTERISTICS AND CROSS-TABULATIONS
34.	Private households with usual residents	Household composition
35.	Persons usually resident in private households	Household composition x persons economically active, children, adults
	Household heads	Age, marital status x sex
	Persons usually resident in private households	Head's age, marital status, sex
36.	Private households with usual residents aged 16+	No. of adults in household x economic position x no. of children in household
37.	Persons aged 16+ usually resident in private households	Economic position x no. of children in household
	Married females in private households of one married female with one or more married male(s)	Economic position x household with or without children
	Children in private households with one or more married males with one married female with or without others	Economic position of married female
38.	Lone adults resident in private households of one adult with children usually resident	Sex x economic position x household with or without children

63

APPENDIX 6 (cont.)

TABLE	BASE 'POPULATION'	CHARACTERISTICS AND CROSS-TABULATIONS
38. cont.	Children usually resident in private households of one adult with children usually resident	Economic position of lone adult
39.	Private households with usual residents	Type of household, households with persons of pensionable age only x no. of children x tenure of households in permanent buildings, households in non-permanent accommodation
	Children and persons of pensionable age usually resident in private households	Tenure of households in permanent buildings, households in non-permanent accommodation
40.	Private households with dependent child(ren) below the age of 25	Households with one-parent families, households with 3+ children x amenities, density of 1+ per room, in not self-contained accommodation, with no car
	Private households with child(ren)	Lone-adult households, households with 2+ adults, households with 3+ children x amenities, density of 1+ per room, in not self-contained accommodation with no car
	Persons usually resident in private households with child(ren)	Age x amenities, density of 1+ per room, in not self-contained accommodation, with no car
41.	Private households with person(s) of pensionable age	Household composition x amenities, tenure, density of 1+ per room, in not self-contained accommodation, with no car
	Persons usually resident in private households with person(s) of pensionable age	Age x amenities, tenure, density of 1+ per room, in not self-contained accommodation, with no car
Welsh Language (Wales only)		
42.	Population usually resident aged 3+	Speak, read, write Welsh x age x speak English
	Population present aged 3+	Speak, read, write Welsh x speak English
PART 2 (10% TABLES)		
43.	Pop. usually resident, 16+ in employment	Industry x age, working outside district of residence x sex
44.	Pop. usually resident, 16+ in employment	Socio-economic group, working outside district of residence x working full-time, part-time.
45.	Persons aged 16+ usually resident in private households	Cars per household x means of travel to work, working full-time, part-time, outside district of residence
46.	Pop. usually resident, economically active or retired	Socio-economic group x economic position x sex x marital status (women)
47.	Private households with usual residents	Socio-economic group of active and retired head, never-active head x tenure of households in permanent buildings, with no car; retired heads x socio-economic group
	All persons and persons economically active usually resident in private households	Tenure of households in permanent buildings, with no car, in households with retired head
48.	Private households with usual residents	No. of families, family type x tenure of households in permanent buildings, with no car

64

TABLE	BASE 'POPULATION'	CHARACTERISTICS AND CROSS-TABULATIONS
49.	Private households with usual residents	Social class of economically active heads, retired and never-active heads
	Persons usually resident in private households	All persons, married females, children, persons aged 65+ x social class of economically active heads, retired and never-active heads
50.	Persons aged 16+ usually resident in private households	All males, males aged 16-64, marital status (women) x social class of economically active persons, retired and never-active persons
51	Population usually resident	Country of birth x sex

APPENDIX 7: CENSUS 1981 : OPCS COUNTY, PARLIAMENTARY
CONSTITUENCY, WARD and CIVIL PARISH MONITORS

I   COUNTY MONITORS

(all data given at County and District level except where indicated)

A.   Population present on census night: change and density
     Population present: 1961, 1971, 1981
     Percentage increase or decrease: 1961-71, 1971-81
     Area (hectares): 1981
     Persons per hectare: 1981

B.   Usually resident population, 1971-81
     1971 total
     1981: Total, males, females
     Percentage increase or decrease (total): 1971-81

C.   Population by age
     Usually resident population:
          Total
          ·Percentage aged: 0-4, 5-15, 16-24, 25-34, 35-44, 45 and under
              pensionable age, all of pensionable age, 75+ men, 75+ women
     Population present on census night:
          same age groups, County only, 1971, 1981

D.   Selected characteristics of the population
     Usually resident population
          Total
          Percentage:
          - in communal establishments
          - living alone
          - born outside United Kingdom
          - in households with head born in New Commonwealth or Pakistan
     Percentage of usually resident children under sixteen in households
     containing only one person aged 16 or over
     Percentage of usually resident pensioners living alone

E.   Economic characteristics of men aged 16-64
     Usually resident population:
          Total men aged 16-44
          Percentage of men aged 16-44
          - economically active
              in employment: full-time, part-time
              out of employment
          - economically inactive
              total
              full-time students
     Population present on census night, 1971
          as above (no distinction full-time/part-time); County only

F.   Economic characteristics of women aged 16-59
     Usually resident population:
          Total women aged 16-59
              as Table E, plus
              percentage of married women aged 16-59 who were
              economically active

66

APPENDIX 7 (cont.)

F. (cont.)
     Population present on census night, 1971
        as above, County only

G. Private households with usual residents: household composition
     Total private households with usual residents
     Number and percentage of households with
     - at least one child aged under five
     - three or more dependent children
     - only one person aged 16 or over plus one or more children under 16
     - one person living alone
     - one pensioner living alone
     - two or more pensioners living alone

H. Housing tenure, amenities and availability of car
     Total private households with usual residents
     Percentage of households
     - owner-occupied
     - rented from council or new town
     - rented from private landlord, housing association, with a job
       or business
     - not in self-contained accommodation
     - with more than 1.0 persons per room
     - lacking or sharing use of a bath
     - with no car
     Private households with persons present on census night
     - as above, County only

Notes
  (i) Urban 'special area' issues give same data at ward level for certain
      inner urban areas
 (ii) County Monitor: Greater London and the Metropolitan Counties gives
      similar data for those units
(iii) County Monitor: Wales: County Summary gives similar data at county
      level, plus 'percentage of persons present aged 3 and over speaking
      Welsh'
 (iv) Scottish Regional Bulletin series give same data (excluding percentage
      in households with NCWP head) for Regions and Districts
  (v) OPCS Monitor: Great Britain: National and Regional Summary (in the
      County Monitor series) gives similar data (excluding Table B) for:
      G.B., England and Wales, England, Regions of England, Metropolitan
      Counties, Regional remainders, Wales, Scotland, Clydeside Conurbation,
      Remainder of Scotland

II PARLIAMENTARY CONSTITUENCY MONITORS

One per region of England; South East split into: Greater London, Remainder
north of Thames, Remainder south of Thames; Scotland, Wales. Data similar
to those in County Monitors for each Parliamentary constituency (Two series,
one for 1981 and one for 1983 constituencies)

III WARD AND CIVIL PARISH MONITORS
STANDARD TABLE

(All data given at County, District, Ward and Civil Parish levels)

Population present on census night:
    1971, 1981, percentage increase or decrease 1971-81
    Area (hectares), persons per hectare 1981
Usually resident population:
    Total, males, females
    Percentage aged under 16
    Percentage of pensionable age
    Number in private households
    Percentage in households with head of household born in NCWP
Percentage of usually resident economically active men aged 16-64
  out of employment
Households with usual residents:
    Number
    Percentage: owner-occupied; rented from council or new
      town; with a car

APPENDIX 8: THE OPCS CENSUS MONITOR SERIES

CEN	78/1	1981 Census: introducing Census Monitors
	78/2	1981 Census of Population: Small Area Statistics (SAS)
	78/3	1981 Census of Population: publication of White Paper
	78/4	1981 Census of Population: developing a question of ethnic origin
	78/5	1981 Census of Population
	78/6	1981 Census of Population
CEN	79/1	1979 Test Census
	79/2	1981 Census of Population
	79/3	1981 Census of Population
	79/4	1981 Census of Population
CEN	80/1	Plans for the 1981 Census
	80/2	Tests of an ethnic question
	80/3	The government's decision on an ethnic question in the 1981 census
	80/4	Parliamentary debates on the draft Census Order
	80/5	Dwellings - 1981 Census
	80/6	1981 Small Area Statistics (SAS): recent progress and announcement of changes
	80/7	1981 Small Area Statistics: final design
	80/8	1981 Census Small Area Statistics: Prospectus
CEN	81/1	Census Day: 5 April 1981
	81/2	The Census taken
	81/3	First results from the 1981 Census
	81/4	1981 Census of Population: first detailed county results published
	81/5	1981 Small Area Statistics: first counties available
CEN	82/1	County Reports from the 1981 Census: publication begins
	82/2	1981 Census: results of the coverage check
	82/3	Evaluation of the 1981 Census
	82/4	1981 Census: 18 months on
CEN	83/1	Census Results: latest progress
	83/2	Population figures from the 1981 Census
	83/3	The range of results broadens
	83/4	Evaluation of the 1981 Census: Post Enumeration Survey
	83/5	1981-1991
	83/6	Evaluation of the 1981 Census: the 10 per cent sample
CEN	84/1	Evaluation of the 1981 Census: demographic comparisons
	84/2	Census results near completion
	84/3	Evaluation of the 1981 Census: Post Enumeration Survey (Quality Check)

Note: Issues labelled '1981 Census of Population' contain a variety of items; other issues often contain items additional to those in their titles.

APPENDIX 9: OPCS MONITOR SERIES

AB	Abortion statistics
DH1	Mortality statistics
DH2	Mortality statistics: cause of death
DH3	Mortality statistics: perinatal and infant
DH4	Mortality statistics: accidents and violence
DH5	Mortality statistics: area
EL	Electoral statistics
FM	Birth statistics
FM2	Marriage and divorce statistics
FM3	Adoption statistics
GHS	General household survey
LFS	Labour force survey
MB1	Cancer statistics
MB2	Communicable disease statistics
MB3	Congenital malformation statistics
MB4	Hospital in-patient enquiry
MN	Migration statistics
PP1	Population estimates
PP2	Population projections (national)
PP3	Population projections (sub-national)
SS	Social surveys
VS	Vital statistics
WR	Registrar-General's weekly returns

APPENDIX 10: THE OPCS 'CENSUS TOPICS' SERIES

1.	Why do we need a census?
2.	The Census in the U.K.
3.	The legal basis
4.	How the census is taken
5.	The questions and how the answers are used
6.	Census results
7.	Census processing
8.	Census confidentiality
9.	The history of the census
10.	Finding the people who count
11.	How to obtain census results

APPENDIX 11: SAS 1971/81 CHANGE FILE TABLES

CF 1   71/81   All persons present

ALL PRESENT	1
Visitors resident in GB	2
Visitors resident outside GB	3
In private households	4
Present residents	5
Not in private households	6
Present residents	7

CF 2   71/81   All persons present not in private households

Establishments	All persons		Resident staff		Other residents	
	Males	Females	Males	Females	Males	Females
TOTAL	8	16	24	32	40	48
Hotels/boarding houses	9	17	25	33	41	49
Children's homes	10	18	26	34	42	50
Old people's homes	11	19	27	35	43	51
Psychiatric hospitals	12	20	28	36	44	52
Other hospitals	13	21	29	37	45	53
Schools and colleges	14	22	30	38	46	54
Other establishments	15	23	31	39	47	55

CF 3   1981 ONLY   All persons present plus absent residents

All absent residents	56
All absent residents in private households	57
All visitors in private households	58

All residents 1981	59
Males in private households	60
Females in private households	61
Persons not in private households	62

CF 4A   71/81   All persons present

Ages	Males	Females
0 - 4	63	65
5 - 15	64	66

CF 4B   71   All persons present
**   81   All residents**

Ages	Males	Females
0 - 4	480	484
5 - 9	481	485
10 - 14	482	486
15	483	487

CF 5   71/81   All persons present

Ages	Persons present
16-24	67
16+	68

Notes:

Source			
CF1	1971	T.1 ;	1981 T.1
CF2	1971	T.1 ;	1981 T.3
CF2	1981	T.1 NB	These counts provide denominators
CF4A	1971	T.4 ;	1981 T.6
CF4B	1971	T.4 ;	1981 T.2
CF5	1971	T.4, T.6 and T.7 ;	1981 T.6

APPENDIX 11 (Cont)

CF6 71 All persons present in private households
CF8 81 All residents in private households

Age	Males SWD	Males Married	Females SWD	Females Married
TOTAL	69	84	98	113
0-14	70	-	99	114
15-19	71	85	100	115
20-24	72	86	101	116
25-29	73	87	102	117
30-34	74	88	103	118
35-39	75	89	104	119
40-44	76	90	105	120
45-49	77	91	106	121
50-54	78	92	107	122
55-59	79	93	108	123
60-64	80	94	109	124
65-69	81	95	110	125
70-74	82	96	111	126
75+	83	97	112	

*1971

CF9 71 All persons present economically active
81 All economically active residents

Ages	Males SWD	Males Married	Females SWD	Females Married
TOTAL	171		185	199
15-19*	172		186	200
16-19				
20-24	173		187	201
25-29	174		188	202
30-34	175		189	203
35-39	176		190	204
40-44	177		191	205
45-49	178		192	206
50-54	179		193	207
55-59	180		194	208
60-64	181		195	209
65-69	182		196	210
70-74	183		197	211
75+	184		198	212

*1971

OPCS Crown Copyright Reserved

Notes

Source CF6 1971 T.7 ; 1981 T.21 ; CF9 1971 T.5 ; 1981 T.9
        CF7 1971 T.7 ; 1981 T.6   ; CF10 1971 T.5 ; 1981 T.5
        CF8 1971 T.6 ; 1981 T.6   ; CF11 1971 T.7 ; 1981 T.20

CF7 71/81 All persons present in private households

Age	Males	Females
TOTALS	127	138
0-14*	128	139
0-15		
15-24*	129	140
16-24		
25-34	130	141
35-44	131	142
45-54	132	143
55-59	133	144
60-64	134	145
65-69	135	146
70-74	136	147
75+	137	148

*1971

CF8 71/81 All persons present not in private households

Marital status and ages	Males	Females
SWD	149	151
Married	150	152
0-24	153	162
25-34	154	163
35-44	155	164
45-54	156	165
55-59	157	166
60-64	158	167
65-69	159	168
70-74	160	169
75+	161	170

CF10 71 All persons present economically active (aged 15 and over)
81 All economically active residents (aged 16 and over)

Economic position	Males	Females SWD	Females Married
Working	213	215	217
Seeking work and sick	214	216	218

CF11 71 All persons present in private households (aged 15 and over)
81 All residents in private households (aged 16 and over)

Economic position	Males SWD	Males Married	Females SWD	Females Married
Working	219	222	225	228
Seeking Work and sick	220	223	226	229
Economically inactive	221	224	227	230

CF12 71 All persons present in private households (aged 15 and over)
     81 All residents in private households (aged 16 and over)

Persons economically active (EA)	231

CF13 71 All persons present not in private households (aged 15 and over)
     81 All residents not in private households (aged 16 and over)

Economic position	Males		Females	
	SWD	Married	SWD	Married
Working	232	235	238	241
Seeking work and sick	233	236	239	242
Economically inactive	234	237	240	243

CF14 71 All present residents
     81 All residents

Country of birth	Males	Females
England	244	258
Scotland	245	259
Wales	246	260
Rest of UK	247	261
Irish Republic	248	262
Old Commonwealth	249	263
New Commonwealth and Pakistan	250	264
Africa	251	265
America	252	266
India	253	267
Pakistan/Bangladesh	254	268
Far East/Ceylon	255	269
Mediterranean	256	270
Other European	257	271

CF15 71/81 Private households with persons present; persons present in households
     1981 ONLY Private households with residents; household residents

Households with persons present	272
Households with residents (1981 ONLY)	273
Persons present in households	278
Residents in households (1981 ONLY)	279
71/81 Household spaces	274
Households absent	

71 Private households present; persons present in households
81 Private households with residents; household residents

Households with - 1 car	275
- 2 or more cars	276
- No car	277
Persons in households with - 1 car	280
- 2 or more cars	281
- No car	282

CF16 71/81 Rooms in absent households
     Rooms in hotels and boarding houses

	Total Rooms
Absent households	283
Hotels and boarding houses	284

Notes

Source   CF12   1971 T.7 ; 1981 T.20
         CF13   1971 T.6 ; 1981 T.5 and T.20
         CF14   1971 T.8; 1981 T.4
         CF15   1971 T.15; 1981 T.11, T.12 and T.17
         CF16   1971 T.17; 1981 T.11

APPENDIX 11 (Cont)

CF17 71 Private households present; rooms in such households; persons present in households
81 Private households with residents; rooms in such households; household residents

Number of persons	Number of rooms						TOTAL	Total rooms
	1 or 2	3	4	5	6	7+		
ALL HOUSEHOLDS	285	294	303	312	321	330	339	348
1	286	295	304	313	322	331	340	349
2	287	296	305	314	323	332	341	350
3	288	297	306	315	324	333	342	351
4	289	298	307	316	325	334	343	352
5	290	299	308	317	326	335	344	353
6	291	300	309	318	327	336	345	354
7+	292	301	310	319	328	337	346	355
TOTAL PERSONS	293	302	311	320	329	338	347	-

CF18 71/81 Private households present

	Households with the following persons							TOTAL
	1	2	3	4	5	6	7+	
(on 1971 pop. base)	356	357	358	359	360	361	362	363

1981 ONLY Private households with residents

	Households with the following persons							TOTAL
	1	2	3	4	5	6	7+	
1981 (1981 pop. base) NB Counts 472 to 479 provide denominators	472	473	474	475	476	477	478	479

CF19 71 Private households (H) present; persons (P) present in households
81 Private households (H) with residents; persons (P) resident in households

Tenure		All amenities exclusive	Lack bath	Inside WC		Persons per room		No car
				Share	Lack	Over 1½	Over 1 to 1½	
Owner Occupier	H	364	367	373	379	385	391	397
	P	488	368	374	380	386	392	398
Council, New Town, SSHA	H	365	369	375	381	387	393	399
	P	489	370	376	382	388	394	400
Others	H	366	371	377	383	389	395	401
	P.	490	372	378	384	390	396	402

CF20 71 households (H) present; rooms in such households; persons (P) present in households
81 households (H) with residents; rooms in such households; persons (P) resident in households

Tenure		Households with the following rooms						Total households	Total rooms
		1 or 2	3	4	5	6	7+		
Non-permanent buildings	H	403	411	419	427			447	455
	P	404	412	420	428			448	-
Owner Occupier	H	405	413	421	429	435	441	449	456
	P	406	414	422	430	436	442	450	-
Council, New Town, SSHA	H	407	415	423	431	437	443	451	457
	P	408	416	424	432	438	444	452	-
Others	H	409	417	425	433	439	445	453	458
	P	410	418	426	434	440	446	454	-

Notes
CF17	1971	T.19	;	1981	T.14
CF18	1971	T.19	;	1981	T.17
CF19	1971	T.21	;	1981	T.10
CF20	1971	T.19	;	1981	T.13

APPENDIX 11 (Cont)

CF21 71 Private households present; persons present in households
    81 Private households with residents; persons resident in households

Households with:	
No child	459
One child - 0-4	460
- 5-14/15*	461
Two or more children - All 0-4	462
- All 5-14/15*	463
- Others	464
ALL PERSONS IN HOUSEHOLDS	465
Persons E.A.	466

* 5-14 in 1971; 5-15 in 1981

CF22 71 Private households present
    81 Private households with residents

HOUSEHOLDS WITH	
Lone male 65	467
Lone female 60	468
2+ all pensionable	469
1 or more pensioners with 1 non-pensioner	470
1 or more pensioners with 2 or more non-pensioners	471

Notes

CF21 1971 T.20 ; 1981 T.18
CF22 1971 T.20 ; 1981 T.32